Rycroft on Analysis and Creativity

Rycroft on Analysis and Creativity

CHARLES RYCROFT

NEW YORK UNIVERSITY PRESS
Washington Square, New York

First published in the USA in 1992 by
NEW YORK UNIVERSITY PRESS
Washington Square,
New York, NY 10003

Library of Congress Cataloging-in-Publication Data
Rycroft, Charles.
Rycroft on Analysis and Creativity / Charles Rycroft.
p.   cm.
Includes bibliographical references and index.
ISBN 0-8147-7427-X (alk. paper) — ISBN 0-8147-7428-8
(pbk. : alk. paper)
1. Psychoanalysis.   2. Freud, Sigmund, 1856–1939—Influence.
3. Psychoanalysts.   4. Creative ability.   I. Title.
RC509.R94   1992
150.19′5—dc20   91-46353
CIP

Published in the U.K. by The Hogarth Press, an imprint of
Chatto & Windus Ltd., under the title *Viewpoints*

New York University Press books are printed on acid-free paper,
and their binding materials are chosen for strength and durability.

Manufactured in the U.S.A.

c 10 9 8 7 6 5 4 3 2 1
p 10 9 8 7 6 5 4 3 2 1

It is altogether beyond our powers to explain how it should be possible that 'I', the thinking subject, can be the object of perception to myself, able to distinguish myself from myself.

Immanuel Kant

The province of the imagination is to give consciousness to the subject by presenting to it its conceptions objectively.

Samuel Taylor Coleridge

A secret self I had enclos'd within.

Thomas Traherne

Contents

Introduction   1

THOUGHTS ON ANALYSIS

1 Faith, Hope and Charity   9

2 On Anxiety   32

3 Where Is Psychoanalysis Going?   41

4 Why Psychiatry Is an Intrinsically
   Odd Profession   47

5 Model and Metaphor in Psychology   52

FREUD, FELLOWS AND CRITICS

6 Why Freud and Jung Could Never Agree   59

7 A Passionate Friendship –
   Freud and Fliess   62

8 Masson's Assault on Freud   71

9 Freud for Historians   82

10 The Wound and the Bow   86

11 Soul Murder and Survival
   – Bruno Bettelheim   95

12 Szasz and the Myth of
   Mental Illness   103

13 Berne and Games People Play   108

THE CREATIVE SELF

14 Symbolism, Imagination and
    Biological Destiny   113
15 Remembering, Imagining, Creating   126
16 Look Back in Loathing   133
17 Sartre's Vision of Freud   138
18 Rousseau: Man and Superwoman   142
19 On Selfhood and Self-Awareness   147
    Complete Bibliography   163
    Index   175

Introduction

Although this is the third volume of essays that I have published, it is the first time that the task of writing the introduction has fallen on myself. Freed from my predecessors' need to give reasons for recommending me as a writer worth reading, I shall simply restrict myself to a brief account of the nature and provenance of the essays which follow.

In the late 1950s I gradually withdrew from the British Psycho-Analytical Society, largely because I was discomforted by its resistance to any unorthodox views, and decided to devote the time and energies I had previously given to administrative work for the Society to writing for the general public. This change of direction was made easier by the fact that in 1959 I began to review for *The Observer* on matters psychoanalytical. One thing led to another, and by the end of the 1960s I was also writing reviews for *New Society*, the *New Statesman*, *The Times Literary Supplement* and the *New York Review of Books*. At the same time I was giving occasional lectures and talks, often to the psychiatric departments of teaching hospitals, and writing books which aimed to present psychoanalytical ideas in everyday language and to demystify a subject whose insights were (and still are) all too often obscured by impenetrable jargon.

These activities continue, and the present volume contains nineteen essays written between 1966 and 1990, eleven of which started life as book reviews and six as lectures or contributions to discussions. Of the remaining two, 'Faith, Hope and Charity', appeared in *The Sources of Hope*, edited by Ross Fitzgerald and published in Australia: it discusses the three theological virtues in the light of the psychoanalytical ideas of Erik Erikson and

D. W. Winnicott. The other, 'On Selfhood and Self-Awareness', I wrote while preparing the present volume for publication. This was prompted by a review of a book on self-portraits that I had written for *Modern Painters*, but its seed was sown, I suspect, by a remark my elder daughter made when she was four. She was describing a change that had recently occurred in her and had yet to occur in her younger brother and sister, and did so by saying, 'When I do things I know that I know what I'm doing.'

The essays are presented in three groups. The first group, 'Thoughts on Analysis', consists of pieces in which I speak simply as an analyst and state my opinions on psychoanalytical ideas and on psychoanalysis's problems and future. The second, 'Freud, Fellows and Critics', describes the viewpoints of Freud and Jung, and those of a number of American admirers and critics of Freud – Jeffrey Moussaieff Masson, Peter Gay, Leonard Shengold, Bruno Bettelheim, Thomas Szasz, and Eric Berne. (Here I wear my book reviewer's rather than my psychoanalyst's hat.) The third group, 'The Creative Self', contains essays in which I expound my own views on creativity and its relation to memory, imagination and biological destiny – views which do not accord with either Freud's early view that creative activity is a variant of neurotic fantasy or with the latter-day Kleinian view that it is reparative.

Although much of this book comments on the views of others, I have, of course, a viewpoint of my own. This will, I hope, become clear to readers as they proceed – particularly, perhaps, while reading the third section – but it may be useful if I borrow a procedure from theology and attempt to locate approximately the point or position from which I view things by contrasting it with what it is not.

First of all my standpoint is European not American, inasmuch as I cherish a sense of the past and believe that ideas – and people too – can only be appreciated and understood if one knows their origins and history. As George Eliot said (in *Felix Holt*): 'There is no private life which has not been determined by a wider public life.' But then it is English and not continental, in that I am suspicious of metaphysics and idealist philosophies and feel comfortable in the British empiricist tradition. I remember that in 1967 I was relieved of a nagging sense of guilt at not having read the continental Existentialists by the following sentence from Iris Murdoch's *Sartre*: 'It might even be argued that recent continental philosophers have been discovering, with immense fuss, what the English empiricists have known since Hume, whom Husserl himself claimed as an ancestor'. And when Paul Roazen, reviewing *Psychoanalysis and Beyond*, described a statement of mine that 'Hegel and Nietzsche are not in my bones' as a 'dreadful self-confession', I was not abashed.

Thirdly, it is, through no fault or merit of my own, an Oxbridge perspective, though I should be at a loss to explain exactly what I mean by this. But I suppose that I rather approve of some of the things that Goldsworthy Lowes Dickinson wrote about the Cambridge mind, which Maynard Keynes quoted in his *Essays in Biography*: 'It is a type unworldly without being saintly, unambitious without being inactive, warmhearted without being sentimental. Through good report and ill such men work on, following the light of truth as they see it; able to be sceptical without being paralysed; content to know what is knowable and to reserve judgement on what is not. The world could never be driven by such men, for the springs of action lie deep in ignorance and madness.'

I could apply the same procedure of defining by negatives, to my viewpoint as a psychoanalyst (if that is what I am). It is not classically Freudian, since I do not believe that psychoanalysis is one of the natural sciences and think that authoritarian tendencies lurk within such apparently innocent techniques as insistence upon the couch (as opposed to offering it) and on mandatory sessions five times a week (as opposed to adjusting attendance to fit the patient's expressed needs, wishes and commitments). Nor is it Kleinian, since I do not believe in either innate envy or the Death Instinct. And, much as I admired and liked Winnicott as a person, it is not Winnicottian. His technique was too finely tailored to his own most unusual personality to be safely copied by others, and there is something about his emphasis on 'holding' the patient during regressions, and on the virtues of refraining from interpretation, that induces benign laziness in analysts less gifted than himself.

But having gone so far in saying what I am not, I must add positively that I am an object-relations theory man, inasmuch as I believe that health or illness depends on the vicissitudes of the personal relationships in which the individual engages throughout life from birth onwards. I also believe that the most important advances in psychoanalysis during my professional lifetime have been made by John Bowlby in his magnum opus, *Attachment and Loss* (about which I have written in *Psychoanalysis and Beyond*), and by Gregory Bateson, whose double-bind hypothesis and its ramifications have vastly increased the subtlety with which one can elucidate both past disturbances in personal relationships, and present obstacles to free communication between analyst and patient.

It also seems to me that the various analytical schools all underestimate the role played by emotions, as opposed to drives and wishes, and tend to ignore the fact that, in adult life at least, emotions are rarely the simple ones of anger, desire and grief but are usually highly complex, with not all their complexities being due to ambivalence. Analysts often describe themselves as mirroring the experiences of their patients, but it seems to me that when they do, they should be acting as mirrors with a finer definition than that possessed by the patient's own consciousness. Perhaps, indeed, they should aspire to the ideal of the poet who, according to T. S. Eliot in 'To Criticize the Critic', should make people 'see and hear more at each end (of the ordinary range) than they could ever see without his help' and should feel the 'obligation to explore, to find words for the inarticulate, to capture those feelings which people can hardly even feel because they have no words for them'.

Since I stopped participating in the activities of the British Psycho-Analytical Society, the three charismatic characters who used to dominate it – Anna Freud, Melanie Klein and D. W. Winnicott – have all died and, so far as I can discern from the sidelines, their cloaks have not fallen unequivocally on anyone in particular (though claimants may perhaps be lurking in the wings). This lack of charismatic teachers may in the long run prove to be a blessing – charismatic characters do harm as well as good – but I sometimes feel that many contemporary analysts, who were trained to be followers, look a little lost without a leader.

The time has come for me to make acknowledgements. I pass over the statutory expressions of gratitude to the various analysts who trained and taught me and to the numerous patients from whom I have learnt so much. I also pass over the equally statutory obligation to thank family and friends, who have had the forbearance to suffer gladly the restraints and inconveniences contingent on harbouring a writer in their midst. Instead I should like to thank the various editors who have encouraged me to write for them and have fostered whatever talent I may possess – notably Terence Kilmartin, John Gross, Robert Silvers, Ross Fitzgerald, Paul Barker, Richard Boston, Tony Gould and, more particularly, James Mitchell and Peter Fuller, both of whom have died long before their time and are much missed.

I should like, too, to thank my present editor at Chatto & Windus, Jenny Uglow, for her ability to unscramble long sentences where I have tried to put a quart of meaning into a pint pot. Chatto and The Hogarth Press, with whom I have worked before, always remind me of the sign on a garage near the beginning of the M3, 'nice people to do business with'.

Finally, readers will find that this book eschews footnotes, but short bibliographies are given for the longer pieces, and the published versions of individual essays are noted in the complete bibliography of my writings at the end of the volume.

Charles Rycroft
October 1990

THOUGHTS ON ANALYSIS

I

Faith, Hope and Charity

The first two paragraphs of this essay only make sense if the reader knows that it first appeared in a volume of essays entitled *The Sources of Hope*, published in both Britain and Australia; and that, for some reason, I was at an early age deeply impressed by the fact that Australia is a land where the rains really can fail and rivers dry up.

On rereading it for its present publication I regret that it was not included in my *Psychoanalysis and Beyond*, as it would have helped to clarify what I was getting at in choosing such an apparently pretentious title. This essay shows, I hope clearly, why I think that, like patriotism, psychoanalysis is not enough.

The title of this collection of essays, *The Sources of Hope*, makes two assumptions, neither of which are, to my mind, so self-evident as to be allowed to pass without comment. It assumes, first, that there is such a thing as hope, that it is possible to locate and define some specific mental state called hope, and secondly, that this mental state is of a kind that can be conceived to have sources, i.e. that it has, as rivers do, some place or places of origin from which it begins and from which it takes its sustenance. The implication is clearly that hope is something that only exists contingently, since one can imagine its sources drying up or becoming exhausted; in which event hope would cease and be replaced by a negative condition of hopelessness – which may or may not be the same as despair.

There is, in fact, a metaphor lurking concealed within the title of this book, a metaphor based on the perception or presumption of some similarity between the mental state called hope and those natural objects and artefacts which depend for their existence and functioning on a supply of something coming into them from outside themselves. Rivers are only rivers because they receive water from springs and from the rain that falls on their catchment areas, and, if springs dry up and the rains fail, rivers cease to be rivers: a state of riverlessness supervenes. Automobiles only function as automobiles if they are supplied with their appropriate source of energy, petrol; and historians and literary critics would soon cease to exist as such if they were cut off from their sources.

The idea that hope has sources implies, then, that it is an attribute of some 'open system' which depends upon input, which consumes what it takes in, and which generates activity while doing so. Rivers receive water from springs and rain, and give it to seas, and their energy can be harnessed to mills and hydroelectric stations, cars can be driven places, and historians and literary critics write books and learned papers which, hopefully, others read and are enriched by. So, if the metaphor implicit in the phrase 'sources of hope' is valid, hope is a mental state which has something to do with the maintenance of cyclical processes involving intake and feedback, and, since it is something that can only be attributed literally to living creatures, hope must be a mental state related to the contingencies of life processes; it must refer to some general property of living organisms, which they continue to possess or display as long as they live and without which they cease to do so, but which can be conceived to originate, to have its sources, somewhere other than in the living organism itself. 'While there is life, there is hope' says the proverb, but, as is the wont of proverbs, this one leaves one in doubt – do we hope so long as we live, in which case hope is nothing more than an epiphenomenon of continued life, or do we live so long as we hope, in which case an enquiry into the sources of hope is an enquiry into what it is that makes living creatures go on living? This is, indeed, the precise Sixty-Four Thousand Dollar Question. Is hope simply a word we use to affirm that we are still alive and wish to continue to be so, in

which case its immediate source is our biological energy and its
remoter sources are in the environment from which we derive
our nutriment, or is it something which we need in order to want
to continue to live, in which case its sources are whatever
circumstances, expectations, ideas and beliefs are necessary to
sustain our wish to continue to live? Before, however, even
beginning to discuss which of these two possible general answers
is the correct one – or whether, perhaps, they are not as
antithetical as they seem – it is necessary to consider briefly what
the word 'hope' means.

According to the *Shorter Oxford English Dictionary* hope is
the 'expectation of something desired; desire combined with
expectation', and it is therefore an emotion compounded of two
elements. To hope for something in particular we must both
desire it and have the expectation that our desire may or will be
realized, and to have hope in general we must both have desires
and have expectations that they can or could be realized. And
contrariwise, if we desire nothing or expect that any desire we
might have will not be realized, we will be without hope; in the
first instance, that of being without desire, because we are
beyond or outside hope, in some state of mind in which the
question of hope no longer arises, and in the second instance,
that of being without expectation that any of our desires could
ever be realized, we are hopeless, in the sense of being in despair.

Since hope is compounded of desire and expectation, it is what
Roget's Thesaurus calls a prospective affection, an emotion or
emotional attitude directed towards the future, and its presence
or absence depends on an assessment, which may of course be
incorrect, of what will happen. In this respect it resembles
fearfulness and anxiety, both of which depend on an assessment
of what will happen, and is the opposite of satisfaction, sorrow, regret, remorse and nostalgia, all of which depend on
evaluations of what has happened, of what we have or have not
done.

According to William McDougall, hope is one of a whole class
of 'prospective emotions of desire', which also includes confidence, disappointment, anxiety, despondency and despair, such
emotions differing in the assessment that is being made of the

likelihood of desire being realized. We are confident if we assume blithely that desire will be realized, we are hopeful if we anticipate that it will be realized but appreciate that contingencies could arise to prevent this, we are despondent if we think it unlikely to be realized, we are in despair if we come to believe that our desire never will be realized. And we experience disappointment if we lose all expectation of our desire being realized while still continuing to desire.

It seems to be characteristic of all these prospective emotions that they can exist in both particular and general forms, i.e. that we can feel them either in respect of some particular desire, which we may believe will, may, may not, probably will not, cannot possibly be realized, or about our desires in general, tending to assume that they will, may, may not, will not be realized. In other words, the assessment we make of the future, which determines whether we feel hopeful or not, seems to depend not only on the information available to us about it, but also on how we interpret that information, our interpretation being influenced by both our past experience and by what used to be called our temperament. If Eysenck is right, stable extraverts with a choleric temperament tend to assess the future optimistically, unstable introverts with a melancholic temperament tend to assess it pessimistically, while stable introverts with a phlegmatic temperament view it philosophically and unstable extraverts with a sanguine temperament give it little heed.

Hope, then, is an attitude towards the future, a feeling, emotion about it which includes two features, that we desire something that we do not yet have and that we believe that we could or may gain it. Hope, therefore, occupies a key position between the present and the future. If we had already fulfilled all our desires, we would neither have nor need hope, since the future would no longer have anything to offer us; we would be without hope but not hopeless. But if we still have desires, these desires, unless we have hope, will produce despair – unless we are certain that our desires will be fulfilled, in which case again we will not need hope. As Spinoza said, 'Fear cannot be without hope, nor hope without fear.' Hope is, therefore, a present attitude towards a future known to be intrinsically contingent and uncertain and cannot be attributed to creatures with no sense of futurity or to anyone too unaware to appreciate that the future can never be certain.

Religious Christians, who believe that God is both the source and the end of hope, understand this well. There is no hope in Heaven, since its object, the Beatific Vision, has already been attained; there is no hope in Hell, since the possibility of attaining its object has been finally lost; and until the Gates of Heaven or Hell have been reached, hope, 'confidence in God's goodness, tempered by fear of His justice' (as the *Oxford Dictionary of the Christian Church* defines it), with faith and charity, constitute the three heavenly graces or theological virtues – as opposed to the more secular, worldly cardinal virtues of prudence, temperance, fortitude and justice.

It would appear then that hope, in its general sense, is an attitude of mind towards the future, one which admits that it is uncertain – as, indeed, it always is – but nonetheless envisages the possibility or likelihood that it will include opportunities for the realization of desires. If we are religious, this future about which we may have hope is not in this world or in this life but in Heaven and in the after-life and the source of our hope resides in our faith and charity, but if we are not religious, in the traditional Christian sense, the future for which we may have hope can only be in this world and our sources of hope can only reside in our assessment of what the future will hold – for both ourselves individually and those to whom we are attached and will, we hope, survive us – and in our temperament and personality; or, more precisely, in the dialectical interaction between these two facets of our being, between the prospective vision we have of the, or our, future and the retrospective vision of our past, which constitutes the source of our present conception of ourselves and of our likely future.

It is, I suppose, just necessary to add that both these interacting visions may be untrue. The future may turn out to be very different from what we had expected and may, therefore, surprise us, pleasantly or unpleasantly; and future events may compel us to reassess our conception of our past, to rewrite our biographies to take fuller account of events which we had previously thought trivial or to attach greater importance to aspects of our personality which we had previously disregarded. For instance, some success may force us to admit that we had hoped more for recognition than we had realized, some failure may leave us feeling more disappointed than we had expected. But the point I am making here is that hope is generated at the interface between the past and the future, and is a quality possessed by that Janus-faced entity, our present self.

Our conception of the future into which we expect to move is, rather obviously, a function of the time, place, society and class into which we happen to have been born. In static, rigidly hierarchical societies this conception may seem to be pre-ordained, life being envisaged as a passage through a series of familiar stages down which our ancestors have trodden from time immemorial, and time being envisaged as a circular process in which events recur. Under such circumstances, hope will only arise in connection with those aspects of life in which uncertainty inevitably reigns – we may hope to survive long enough to experience all the preordained stages of life and to avoid such natural disasters as famines, floods and failure of the crops. But hopes contingent on progress and individual freedom will never arise.

In open societies, on the other hand, in which social mobility exists and ideas of individual and social progress are in the air, more complicated and sophisticated hopes will arise, since it will be possible to hope to achieve positions very different and distant from where one started and to attain greater self-awareness, culture and wisdom than one's point of origin automatically granted one. In other words, hope can manifest itself as ambition and aspiration, and fulfilment and disappointment can be experienced in respect of such desires as those for wealth, power, social advancement and professional recognition on the one hand, and those for self-realization, self-knowledge, wisdom and righteousness on the other.

In the liberal democracies, indeed, ambition and aspiration are so inculcated by education that hopes doomed to disappointment are engendered in every child. If success is the ideal to be aimed at, realization of the hopes of the few is, of necessity, purchased at the cost of the failure and disappointment of the many, since the top would not be worth getting to if there were room on it for everyone. This state of affairs is only made tolerable, to the extent that it is, by two things: first, by the fact that some hopes seem to fade away or be replaced by others without leaving behind them scars of bitterness and disappoint- ment; and, secondly, by the fact that society is complex enough to grant failures in one sphere of life success in another. I doubt whether many of the thousands of girls who hope to become ballerinas, or boys who hope to play in a Test Match, or Americans who hope to become President of the United States, are permanently traumatized by their failure to achieve these ambitions, and, as Geoffrey Gorer has pointed out, one of the advantages of complex societies containing several élites is that they provide a variety of socially recognized hierarchical ladders, so that ambitious people who aspire to success can achieve it in one area even though they may fail in others.

It remains, however, true, I believe, that where hope manifests itself as ambition and the desire for fame, the success of the few is purchased at the price of creating envy and disappointment in many. Hence, of course, the pleasure many people take in the misfortunes, scandals and downfalls of the famous; and hence too Andy Warhol's presumably ironical prediction that society will eventually be organized to ensure that each of its members enjoys fifteen minutes of fame.

Religious people are, perhaps, fortunate in being able to detach hope from the contingencies of the material future, and from the possibility of disappointment in this world, by the hope of salvation in the next. Although there is no Room at the Top for everyone here, there is room for everyone in Heaven, and if people really are religious their source of hope is not their position in the rat-race but their inner state of mind. The same holds for everyone who has a 'philosophy of life', regardless of how they formulate it; so long as they have some ideal, be it for wisdom, self-realization, understanding, acceptance, or truth, they will be able to transcend and survive adversities and disappointments. Unfortunately too little is known about the psychology of those who have indestructible ideals and are immune to demoralization by disappointments, bereavements, persecution and torture. They do not seek psychotherapeutic help, are not Suitable Cases for Treatment, and, as a result, the origins of their hope, or rather faith, have yet to be located by the psychiatrists and psychoanalysts. But ordinary language asserts that they possess 'inner resources'.

At this point it has become clear to me and will, I suspect, have become clear to some of my readers that there really is some substance in the distinction made by theologians between hope and faith. Hope is for something, be it success, love or the Beatific Vision, and is a contingent emotion, which depends on the individual's expectations, on his assessment of his future seen from the perspective of the experience he has acquired during his past, whereas faith is an absolute, timeless emotion, which one either has or has not independently of whether one has grounds for hope. Theologians, I gather, distinguish between objective faith, 'the Faith believed in' by believers and formulated in creeds, and subjective faith, 'the Faith whereby belief is reached', the former being whatever set of beliefs the religious person holds, the latter being that act or attitude which enables him to hold beliefs.

According to Erik Erikson, who is, so far as I can discover, the only psychoanalyst to mention faith, even in passing, faith is identical with what he calls Trust, which is something that infants acquire in their mothers' arms or not at all. 'Mothers, I think, create a sense of trust in their children by that kind of administration which in its quality combines sensitive care of the baby's individual needs and a firm sense of personal trustworthiness within the trusted framework of their culture's style.' In Erikson's view, then, trust is transmitted from mother to infant in a context and at an age when faith, hope and charity cannot yet be differentiated. When a mother cares for her infant's individual needs in a trustworthy way within a trusted framework, she is both displaying and transmitting the three theological virtues in their most elemental forms.

The neglect of faith by psychoanalysts and psychologists is

paralleled by an equally striking neglect of hope. As John Cohen has put it, 'But although life without hope is unthinkable, psychology without hope is not, judging by the conspicuous absence of any study of hope from the literature.' The Subject Index of Freud's *Collected Works* contains no entries for Faith, Hope, Despair, or Hopelessness, and even McDougall, despite his meticulous phenomenological analysis of hope, is silent about faith.

The reason for this neglect, or rather avoidance, of hope and faith is, I think, twofold. Both psychology and Freudian psychoanalysis claim to be sciences, science is concerned with causes, and causes are always located in the past; there are, therefore, methodological and, indeed, ideological difficulties about the prospective emotions, which depend upon the individual's subjective sense of himself as a continuous entity passing through time into the future. Furthermore, psychoanalysis began as a branch of medicine and its raw material still derives from people who are in trouble and seeking help; it has, therefore, more to say about illness than about health, and a tendency to describe human nature in a terminology derived from pathology. As a result, it has more to say about depression and the schizoid sense of futility than about the faith and hope of the healthy, and more to say about the divisions in the Divided Self than about the self that is liable to become divided.

Psychoanalysis and psychology have, therefore, a retrospective, pathological bias which makes them apter tools for explaining the present in terms of the past than for elucidating the role played by the envisaged future; and for explaining why people may become depressed or despairing in the absence of rational grounds for doing so than why people may continue to have faith and hope in the absence of rational grounds for continuing to have them. In his book *The Informed Heart*, Bruno Bettelheim makes it clear that those inmates of concentration camps who remained undemoralizable were not people who would have satisfied psychoanalytical criteria of normality.

Erikson's equation of faith with trust and his assertion that trust is a quality of mind created and transmitted by good mothering in infancy is, in fact, a good example of the way in which the retrospective bias in psychoanalysis works. If this statement is not only true but also the whole truth, the source of hope is quite simply in the past. If we have had good mothering, we will have faith and hope, and their source will be our unconscious recollection of that good mothering, and any lack of faith, hope and charity from which we may suffer will be classifiable as a neurotic symptom resulting from maternal deprivation in infancy. According to this simple view of the matter, hope is the effect of a prior cause, viz. good mothering, hopelessness is the effect of another prior cause, viz. defects in mothering, and both have been explained without any reference to the future and without any breach in the natural-scientific model constructed and bequeathed by Freud.

But, in fact, this is not what Erikson thinks at all. His heroes have been people like Luther and Gandhi, both of whom were far from normal by Freudian standards, and his writings have been concerned not only with causation but also with problems of meaning and value. And he has even introduced the word 'virtue' into psychoanalysis to describe such 'ego-strengths' as fidelity, love, care and wisdom. Furthermore, as has recently become public knowledge, he has spent his life trying to re-concile or integrate Freudian psychology with Christianity, an activity which has led him to 'rediscover prescientific truths' and, less admirably, 'to blur the extent of his divergence from the psychoanalytical movement', of which he has always been a prominent member. So when Erikson describes trust as arising when mothers minister to their babies' individual needs with 'a firm sense of personal trustworthiness within the trusted frame-work of their culture's style', he is not, I think, referring just to adequate child-care consonant with prevalent pediatric opinion, but also to the transmission of the virtues of faith, hope and charity from one generation to another. If this is right, and personally I think it is, the sources of hope in any single individual reside in his past, present and imagined future rela-tionships with others, from whom he acquires hope and to whom he may give hope, and hope is not simply an individual quality which some people have and others lack but a social, cultural quality, which is engendered within a social, historical matrix and transmitted from one generation to another – in the simplest instance from parents to their children, but also from teachers to their pupils, from political leaders to their followers, from priests to their congregations, and from psychotherapists to their patients.

It was this social matrix of hope that I had in mind when, at the beginning of this essay, I drew attention to the metaphor implicit in this volume's title, which suggests that hope is like a river which only continues to be a river if springs and rain feed it – and that it is an aspect of an open system which depends for its maintenance on an input from outside and in its turn returns feedback to the outside. And to take this metaphor a step further, just as rivers, rain and springs are part of the water cycle that also includes seas and clouds, so too children, pupils, followers, congregations and patients return hope to their parents, teachers, leaders, priests and therapists. Hope is, in fact, something that circulates within that total, wider, system of relationships we call society.

If then, as I am suggesting, hope is a social quality, which is transmitted from individual to individual, from generation to generation, the sources of hope in any particular person are all those relationships which he has had in the past, which he is having in the present, which he envisages having in the future, and which endow his life with meaning and value. At the risk of being over-schematic, I am tempted to say that these past, present and future relationships constitute the sources of some general quality, strength or virtue of which hope is the prospective facet; past relationships being the source of faith, present relationships being the source of charity, and future relationships being the source of hope. It would seem to me too that faith, hope and charity can to a measure substitute for one another, so that if someone has in the past had relationships which have given him faith, have provided him with what psychoanalytical jargon calls 'good internal objects', he will be able to survive and endure without loss of virtue circumstances in which both charity and hope are in short supply; but that if, on the contrary, someone has lacked good relationships in the past and has no 'good internal objects', he will require and demand enormous quantities of charity now and hope for the future.

The latter is the state of affairs with which psychotherapists are professionally most familiar. For instance, a woman whose mother certainly had not ministered sensitively to her individual needs with a firm sense of personal trustworthiness, but had on the contrary palmed her off with a succession of nurses, became depressed when she realized that her marriage had become a desert, but recovered, after a fashion, when she heard the late D. W. Winnicott speaking anonymously on the radio about mothering. She could, she suddenly thought, ring up the BBC, ask for his name and address and become his patient, if she ever became desperate. She cherished this thought for several years, until she eventually did become desperate. She then rang up the BBC, who refused to give her Winnicott's name, and she was later referred to me as a patient through the conventional medical channels. In treatment with me she rapidly developed what the jargon calls an idealized positive transference, following me at a discreet distance wherever I went, and at times developing hysterical loss of voice when I was out of reach at weekends or on holiday, i.e. she would not, could not, talk to anyone other than me. In this patient, and in others too, the absence of faith, of 'good internal objects', led to both an importunate need for a present relationship with me and to an absurd over-exploitation of hope to compensate for her lack of faith and inner resources. Even if her mother never had loved her, and her husband no longer did love her, she had received a sign, in the form of a voice on the radio, that there existed somewhere a man who could mother her and whose patient she could, at some unspecified time in the future, become.

This clinical anecdote, which I have told in order to illustrate the way in which hope can be mobilized to compensate for deficiencies in faith and charity, will have additional point for those readers who are familiar with Winnicott's writings, since they will appreciate that he really did understand about mothers and infants and that my patient was right in supposing that he would have understood her immediately. He also belonged to that school of psychoanalysts which holds that health is dependent on relationships with others ('objects'), not on satisfactory discharges of instinctual tension, and is one of the few analysts to have discussed hope, even if only briefly.

The use, or rather over-use, of hope to compensate for deficiencies in faith is a phenomenon well known to psychoanalysis, which categorizes it as the defence mechanism of idealization. This defence consists in the construction of ideal images which are projected either on to real persons, whose imperfections are denied, or on to ideals and religious or political movements, and is motivated by the need to deny the anger and resentment that has been engendered by past and present frustrations. The hazards associated with idealization are disillusion, which occurs if the idealized object fails too conspicuously to live up to expectations, and transformation into denigration, which occurs if the repression of anger and resentment breaks down. Another patient of mine depicted the conversion of idealization into disillusion and denigration by a dream in which the moon fell out of the sky into a dustbin. I have discussed idealization and disillusion in detail in Chapter 3 of my book *Imagination and Reality*, where I offer an interpretation of a dream dreamt by the Italian poet Giacomo Leopardi fairly soon after he lost his faith. This dream is also about the moon falling out of the sky.

Idealization, disillusion and denigration play an important part in what might be called the social pathology of hope. It would seem that revered rulers and leaders are always at risk of being overthrown by precisely their erstwhile followers, and that religious institutions are recurrently threatened by iconoclastic revolts.

If hope is the prospective aspect of virtue, of the sense of identity, of health, of integrity, of ego-strength – it is difficult to know which term to use – it must bear a functional relationship to age. At the beginning of life there is little past to look back on and a long future to look forward to; at the end of life there is little future to look forward to and a long past to look back on. As a result the health of the young must include hope for the future, both for themselves individually and for the world they envisage themselves entering and becoming a member of, while the health of the old must depend, not on hope for their individual future, but on the wisdom they have acquired during their past and on vicarious hope for those to whom they remain attached – their children, their pupils, and whatever groups they feel themselves to be truly members of. According to Erikson, wisdom is 'the detached and yet active concern with life as with death' and is the reward of 'successful' old age, the punishment of unsuccessful old age being despair, bitterness and disgust. In youth, then, hope predominates, since desires are psychosomatically active and expectations of a future are 'normally' justified, whereas in age hope retreats to a lesser or vicarious position and is replaced by wisdom and serenity.

Having committed myself to the view that hope is a social quality and that each individual's store of it is a function of his relationship with others, it behoves me to say something about the sociology and history of hope, even though I could plead that this is outside my professional competence, which derives from listening to single individuals talking to me about their private hopes and fears, satisfactions and disappointments. But no man is an island, even when he is lying on an analyst's couch, and the stories my patients tell me and the ways they interact with me are, in fact, parts of a social network which has ramifications embracing all the persons they have known, loved and hated – and indeed embracing all the persons whom I have known and who have contributed to my competence to be their analyst. A curious effect of Freud's attempt to construct pyschoanalysis on a scientific model has been to obscure an obvious and yet important fact, viz. that nothing can happen between an analyst and his patient unless they share a language in common, and to share a language in common means to share much more than a collection of words and grammatical conventions; it involves sharing numberless implicit assumptions, allusions and icon-ographic connections and mutual participation in a common cultural heritage – a mutual participation which may be inten-sive if analyst and patient come from similar backgrounds and have had similar educations, but will be more tenuous if either has to use a language that is not his mother tongue.

As a result the relationship between analyst and patient is not, in fact, that of a pure scientist detachedly observing an isolated specimen of the species *homo sapiens*, even though analysts often write as though it were, but a social encounter between two members of the same culture, one of whom has, or claims to have, symptoms, the other of whom has, or claims to have, expertise which will, hopefully, enable him to elucidate the meaning of those symptoms – this expertise consisting of some understanding of symbolism, defence and transference; in other words of how people, when they talk, can mean more than they know they mean, of how people can conceal their true thoughts and feelings even from themselves, and of how people can react to one person as though he were someone else.

The two parties to this microcosmic social unit, in which the multitudinous others of the macrocosm appear only as images or phantoms, differ from one another not only in the fact that one has symptoms and the other, perhaps, has not and the latter has expertise which the former, perhaps, lacks, but also in the fact that their sources of hope differ in both quantity and quality. Although the patient must have some hope, since if he did not he would not stir himself to come for treatment, his sources of hope must be in some way depleted or contaminated, since if they were not he would not need to come for treatment, while the analyst, unless he is a hypocrite or charlatan, must have faith and hope deriving, in the first instance, from his belief in the efficacy or virtue of his professional skills but more fundamentally from the 'sensitive care' and 'personal trustworthiness' he has received from his own analysts and his own parents.

Curiously enough, analysts are well aware of and entirely open about the value of what they have received from their training analysts – a mystique has, indeed, developed within the analytical fraternity analogous to that of the apostolic succession in the Christian Church, according to which virtue is acquired by the lying on of couches instead of by the laying on of hands – but tend to be mute about the value of what they have received from their parents. This is presumably because until recently no one ever became an analyst unless he needed to make a radical break with his past.

What I am suggesting here is that the relationship between an analyst and his patient is a social encounter between two persons, one of whom has already acquired virtue and hope from somewhere, and the other of whom hopes to acquire it from him, that the symbolic interaction they engage in evokes imagery derived from the culture they both share, and that what goes on betweeen them is a microcosmic version of processes that occur in society at large. If I am right about this, the secluded, isolated, apparently individualistic occupation of psychoanalysis does not debar its practitioners from having insights into the social sources of hope.

Acting on this presumption, the first point I want to make is that all societies of any complexity seem to have a tendency to divide themselves into purveyors and recipients of hope, the purveyors being special people – shamans, gurus, priests, psychoanalysts – who receive an esoteric training and are endowed with some sort of 'mana' or charisma by the others and who may or may not themselves privately believe in the superior qualities attributed to them. In Europe the traditional purveyors of hope were the Church and the aristocracy. The former were entrusted with the 'cure of souls' and were trained in special knowledge of the road to salvation. The latter were entrusted with defence of the realm and, as Peter Laslett has pointed out, acted as symbols of continuity in a world in which life was for most people nasty, brutish and short. Royalty, in particular, was endowed with, and believed itself to have, therapeutic powers. Charles II is believed to have touched 100,000 persons for the King's Evil (scrofula) during his reign, and a form of service for touching was included in the Book of Common Prayer until 1719. Both the Church and the aristocracy demanded of their members privations during their training which modern man would consider inhuman, in return for which they were rewarded with privilege and deference. And both officiated at ceremonials which affirmed the reality and meaning of the realm, of its past and of its future.

Although traces of this theocratic, aristocratic system of

supplying hope and a sense of social cohesion still survive, particularly perhaps in Great Britain, they are anachronistic anomalies, since the idea that society should be divided officially and visibly into two groups, one special, privileged and deserving of deference, the other ordinary and deferential, is deeply offensive to the democratic ideal, which asserts that all men are born equal and regards as mere mythology the ideologies that once sustained the Church and Crown. I doubt, for instance, whether many readers of this book can accept as a sober fact, rather than as an absurd or perhaps endearing fiction, the idea that our Queen is a Fountainhead of Honour (and is the source of another virtue) and derives her capacity to be so from her anointment with oil at her coronation, as a result of which she has been infused with Divine Grace. And yet this is what almost all men did believe until the Enlightenment and the Age of Reason. Nor do many people nowadays believe that genealogies can be invoked as evidence of personal superiority, as aristocrats once openly did.

However, despite the fact that these traditional means by which European societies used to maintain their sense of social cohesion and affirm their beliefs in their past and their hopes for the future have become obsolescent if not obsolete, the need for purveyors of hope still remains and a tendency to create inspiring élites can still be discerned in the modern world. In Communist countries the Party performs this role quite openly, but in the liberal democracies the impulse to hive off a section of the population into a special élite of purveyors of hope manifests itself clandestinely and hypocritically by the creation of two classes of people, one of which satisfies that aspect of hope that can be appeased by idealization, hero worship and identification, the other of which is paid to provide hope.

The former class consists of those people who are correctly styled stars – pop stars, film stars, football stars, even, in England at least, hairdressers and newscasters – whose lives are followed as avidly as those of royalty ever were and whose deaths, which are often premature and tragic (e.g. Marilyn Monroe, James Dean, Elvis Presley), lead to mass demonstrations of grief, which is only assuaged when a new star appears in the firmament. Such people purvey pseudo-hope, since their appeal is, as Erik Erikson again has shown, primarily to people who have yet to discover their own identity and therefore 'over-identify, to the point of apparent complete loss of identity, with the heroes of cliques and crowds'. The stars themselves are, I think, better regarded as victims than as exploiters of society, since they pay a heavy price emotionally for the adulation they receive and the money they and their promoters earn. And they may at any time, if they make a false move, be thrown off their pedestals and into the dustbin.

The second class, those who are paid to provide care and hope, comprise the counselling professions – the psychiatrists, psychotherapists, social workers and probation officers. As Paul Halmos has shown in his book *The Faith of the Counsellors*, these professions practise a benign form of double-think. They purport to provide professional services and skills based firmly on scientific principles derived from psychology and sociology, which they apply 'non-directively' and 'non-judgmentally', when in fact they provide concern, love and hope and are actuated by faith – though what the faith is in is never articulated. Society colludes in, and indeed encourages, this double-think, by treating the counsellors as ordinary professional people, paying them salaries and fees for their technical skills and providing them with career structures, but at the same time covertly endowing them with extraordinary miraculous powers, particularly that of being able to give hope to hopeless cases, and delegating to them the responsibility for making decisions about matters that are moral not scientific. In England at least, the onus for deciding whether a pregnant woman *should* have an abortion falls on psychiatrists, and drug addiction, which is surely a symptom of social malaise and not of physical illness, is treated by psychiatrists, none of whom receive any training in ethics or sociology and only a minority of whom receive any training in psychotherapy. In other words, they are expected to make moral decisions and to provide hope for the despairing, while pretending that they are exercising professional skills derived from their scientific knowledge, a state of affairs only relished by those pyschiatrists who enjoy playing God. Social workers are similarly expected to deal with the consequences of poverty and bad housing as though they were illnesses amenable to treatment, and not surprisingly many of them fortify themselves by becoming believers in psychoanalysis or Marxism. In his book *The Triumph of the Therapeutic*, Philip Rieff has described a similar tendency in the United States to regard all human problems as illnesses amenable to treatment by scientific experts. The elevtion of psychoanalysts to guru status is another example of the same collusive process.

The assumption underlying this development is that faith, hope and charity are commodities that can be bought and sold in the marketplace or provided by the State, and that it is possible to train people in techniques which will make them competent purveyors of them. As Halmos has pointed out, this emergence of a special class of counsellors implies that society is throwing up people who have hope in the future, who believe that science is the only ideology that can be invoked to justify action, and who are disillusioned with politics. It also implies a widespread assumption that it is not the responsibility of each individual to develop his own virtues – as it would be if the liberal democracies really were democracies in which all men are equals and opportunities to achieve the good life really were open to all.

The second point I wish to make is that the traditional symbols of hope seem to have lost their virtue, without having as yet been replaced by any new set of efficacious ones. If science really had proved, as many people nowadays believe, that religion is an illusion, that all rituals and ceremonials are obsessional symptoms, that love is nothing more than a technique for relieving instinctual tension, that all behaviour is motivated by infantile causes, that all virtues and achievements can be interpreted reductively, that all human relationships are games people play, that social activity is role-playing and play-acting, then life really would be a racket and the world really would be a Wasteland in which all that one could do would be to wait for Godot or search for exotic sources of hope in Eastern philosophies or psychedelic drugs.

But, in fact, as anyone who actually bothers to read his Freud, or his Eric Berne, or even his Erving Goffman, will discover, all

these disillusioning, corrosive ideas are either misunderstand-
ings and over-simplifications of what they said – or are examples
of people foisting their personal attitudes to life on to the world
as though they were conclusions to which their scientific researchers had led them. For instance, Eric Berne believed that
people can achieve awareness, spontaneity and intimacy and
that, if they do so, they stop playing games, but one has to
persevere to the last chapter of his *Games People Play* to
discover that he did so. And Freud believed that religion is an
illusion long before even a glimmering of psychoanalysis entered
his mind, having been brought up by free-thinking parents
against whom he did not rebel.

What seems to have happened is that the psychological and
social sciences, flying the flags of Reason and Science, explored
territory where angels fear to tread without appreciating the
symbolic havoc they were creating. The main victims of this
havoc have been, I think, the children of people who in the 1920s
to 1940s were marginally influenced by progressive, enlightened, rationalist ideas; they have had transmitted to them
symbols of hope and virtue which, if modern, are half-baked
and, if traditional, are half-decayed. As many observers have
pointed out, young people who drop out, take off, make the
pilgrimage to Katmandu, become flower children or devotees of
Krishna Consciousness, are usually children of middle-class
parents whose lives have been moral compromises. And in Great
Britain they are grandchildren of people whose belief in progress
or the natural order of things was shattered by the First World
War.

Finally, I must say something about the effects on modern man
of the fact that he is living in an epoch overshadowed by the
possibility that the human race may be about to annihilate itself,
either directly and in one move by nuclear warfare, or more
insidiously and yet inexorably by exhausting its sources of
energy and disturbing the ecological balance between man and
nature. If it were certain that such a man-made end of the human
race was nigh, hope for Humanity as a whole would, indeed, dry
up, since there would cease to be any expectation of any future in

which desires could be satisfied; and the best any single individual could hope for would be that the cataclysm might be postponed until after his own natural death. This is, in fact, a position that some people do adopt; it leads to a curious coalescence of hope and despair, which entitles them to fiddle while Rome burns and to make hay while the sun shines, 'for tomorrow we die'. It is a stance which people, particularly older people, who do not share it are apt to consider cynical or decadent, but is, I think, better regarded as courageous, as the re-emergence of an epic virtue in a world that is apparently affluent and secure. (The epic virtues of courage, heroism and endurance seem to flourish under conditions of scarcity, in which life is, and is known to be, nasty, brutish and short, while the religious and romantic virtues can only flourish under conditions of prosperity and security, in which there is time and leisure for meditation, self-exploration and dalliance. The present state of affairs is anomalous, in that security and affluence coexist with widespread awareness that life could come to an end at any moment. What kinds of virtue flourish under such conditions?)

But in fact it is not certain that the world is coming to an end, with either a bang or a whimper, since the reasons why it is at risk are all man-made and counter-measures are therefore, in principle, possible. Whether they will be taken, and whether the risks really are as great as they are often presented as being, are matters for prediction; and predictions depend upon extrapolations from present facts – in this case, from political facts about the policies and intentions of governments possessing nuclear weapons, from technological facts about resources and their utilization, and from demographic facts about population trends. Discussion of these facts, and of the predictions being made based on them, certainly is outside my professional competence. It belongs, in any case, to an essay on the grounds, not sources, of hope, so I shall confine myself to a few general comments.

First, predictions are not always accurate, and actions based on them are acts of faith not reason, since it is possible to collect examples of predictions based on all the available evidence which have proved wildly wrong. In the 1930s all the evidence suggested that the population of the United Kingdom would fall to 35 million by 1970, but in fact it rose to over 55 million, which was an increase of 9 million as opposed to the estimated decrease of 11 million. In any case, human behaviour is influenced by the predictions that are made about it, since they alter the assessments that are made of the likely future and evoke reactions based on suggestibility and counter-suggestibility.

Secondly, predictions are inevitably based on those facts that are known and cannot take account of facts that are not yet known. For instance, estimates of energy resources can only be based on sources that have already been located and cannot take account of those that have yet to be located. And as there are, of necessity, more not fewer things in this world than have yet been observed, predictions of resources have an inherent tendency to be underestimates. British nuclear energy policy after the last war, for instance, was based on an underestimate of how much coal there was under Britain and complete ignorance that there was any natural gas under its waters.

Thirdly, gloomy predictions circulate more thoroughly than cheerful ones do, just as bad news travels faster than good news and disasters make better headlines than continuing felicities. As a result the information on which we base our expectations of the future is contaminated by a factor which derives, not from the future as it can be rationally assessed, but from that present boredom, discontent and malice which makes prospects of disaster exciting and fascinating. Just as people can maliciously enjoy other people's misfortunes and take a delight in spreading alarm and despondency, so the prospect of universal cataclysm can have its charms. And just as faith, hope and charity generate millennial, utopian and progressive ideals, so envy, hatred and malice generate catastrophic hopes.

Finally, as I have no wish to end this essay on an unduly optimistic note, I must say something about the effects of disseminating the idea that the world is over-populated. Although this may well be true and it may be necessary to discourage births, it has, I think, to be recognized that it is an intrinsically demoralizing idea which strikes at one of the basic biological sources of hope, the belief that fecundity is virtuous:

that one's own birth added an asset to the world and procreation increases the store of goodness. 'Be fruitful, and multiply, and replenish the earth, and subdue it' is one of the oldest and most elemental injunctions, and the present must be the first time that humanity has had to consider the possibility that its success in subduing the earth, combined with its failure to replenish it, may compel it to enjoin its members to be sterile and avoid multiplication. I find it hard to see how we could elevate contraceptive competence to one of the cardinal virtues and turn births into occasions for reproach and condolence, without threatening the self-assurance of both men and women and contaminating the river of hope at its physical sources. A world in which we had not only learned to live with the Pill but also to love it would form a suitable subject for an Erewhonian novel.

1979

Eric Berne, *Games People Play* (London: Methuen, 1965).
Bruno Bettelheim, *The Informed Heart* (London: Thames & Hudson, 1961).
John Cohen, *Humanistic Psychology* (London: Allen & Unwin, 1965).
Erik Erikson, *Childhood and Society* (New York: Norton, 1953).
    Young Man Luther (London: Faber & Faber, 1959).
H. J. Eysenck, *Fact and Fiction in Psychology* (Harmondsworth: Penguin Books, 1965).
Geoffrey Gorer, *The Danger of Equality* (London: Cresset, 1966).
Paul Halmos, *The Faith of the Counsellors* (London: Constable, 1965).
R. D. Laing, *The Divided Self* (London: Tavistock, 1960).
Peter Laslett, *The World We Have Lost* (London: Methuen, 1965).
William McDougall, *An Introduction to Social Psychology*, 22nd edition (London: Methuen, 1931).
Philip Rieff, *Freud: The Mind of the Moralist* (London: Gollancz, 1959).
    The Triumph of the Therapeutic (London: Chatto & Windus, 1966).
Paul Roazen, *Erik H. Erikson: The Power and the Limits of a Vision* (New York: The Free Press, 1976).
Charles Rycroft, *Imagination and Reality* (London: The Hogarth Press, 1968).
R. W. Southern, *The Making of the Middle Ages* (London: Hutchinson, 1953).
Benedict Spinoza, 'The Origin and Nature of the Emotions', in *Spinoza's Ethics*, ed. A. Boyle (London: Dent (Everyman), 1960).
D. W. Winnicott, *Collected Papers* (London: Tavistock, 1958).

2

On Anxiety

I gave this lecture to the Department of Psychotherapy, St George's Hospital, Tooting. As most of the audience were learning to become psychotherapists and some, I could safely assume, were themselves being analysed, I tried to avoid both jargon and controversial issues and confined myself to stating in everyday language a basic schema into which the eleven different kinds of anxiety described in the learned literature could all be fitted.

Anxiety could, I think, claim to be the central concept of all psychoanalytical thinking. Freud says somewhere that it lurks behind every symptom, and any historical account of Freudian theory has to bear in mind the fact that at different stages of his career Freud held three different theories of anxiety, while the author of the 1968 *Critical Dictionary of Psychoanalysis* found it necessary to list eleven different kinds of anxiety – in retrospect it is clear that he could have added a few more. Anxiety is in fact one of those concepts which at first sight seem simple, clear and obvious – after all, we have all been anxious and know all too well what it feels like – but which on further reflection turn out to have unexpected ambiguities and ramifications.

The first ambiguity about anxiety is that it is a symptom, and often an extremely distressing one, but no one in his senses would ever wish to be totally immune to it, no more than anyone would ever wish to be totally immune to pain. If we were totally immune to pain, we would be at continuous risk of being burnt, bruised and fractured; if we were totally immune to anxiety we would be at continuous risk from both physical and psychological dangers. This rather obvious point does, I think, need to be made, perhaps even stressed, since popular, simplified accounts of psychoanalysis and psychotherapy do sometimes imply that some ideal state of being 'anxiety-free' is both attainable and desirable.

A second ambiguity stems from the modern tendency (which derives in fact from psychoanalytical and psychiatric thinking) to define anxiety as 'irrational fear'. This obscures the fact that it is not just an unpleasant emotion occurring now, in the present, but is also what used to be called a 'prospective affection' – an emotion deriving from some uncertainty about what may or will happen in the future. In *Anxiety and Neurosis* (1968) I argued that anxiety is not essentially a form of fear aroused by an inappropriate object or stimulus, but a particular variety of what biologists call vigilance.

In order to survive, all organisms, including of course man, have to be continuously alert to the possibilities of changes in their environment, so that they can avoid dangers and seize opportunities. Their sense-organs, their nervous systems and, in man, their psyches, have to perform the function of an ever-vigilant sentinel. Now it can and, indeed, obviously on occasion does happen that our ever-vigilant sentinel perceives some change in our environment the nature of which cannot as yet be ascertained. Or to put the matter in more human terms, we perceive something which makes us envisage, imagine, foresee, predict some future event the significance of which cannot as yet be assessed, and to which therefore there can as yet be no possible appropriate response. Under such circumstances we become hyper-vigilant, poised to act but unable to react adaptively by fight, flight or submission, or to respond with fear or relief, pleasure or distress, joy or sorrow. This state of being hyper-vigilant, of expecting something as yet unknown, of being poised to experience some emotion without knowing what that emotion is going to be, is, I believe, the essence of anxiety.

I must give an example of what I mean. In the days when I still had to sit for examinations, it always seemed to me that there were two moments of maximal anxiety. One was *after* one had entered the examination hall but *before* one had read the questions listed on the examination paper; as soon as one had read the questions, anxiety ceased and was replaced by either hopeful fight or by despair. The other was as one approached the notice board bearing the examination results but *before* one had discovered whether one's name was on the pass list. As soon as one had found one's name on the list or had ascertained that it was not there, the anxiety ceased and was replaced by either elation or disappointment.

Similarly, anxiety about one's own or someone else's illness seems to hinge on uncertainty of prognosis. If the prognosis is known to be good, anxiety is relieved though concern remains. If the prognosis is hopeless, anxiety is replaced by sorrow and grief.

So far I have been talking about normal, everyday anxiety, but the same principle applies also to neurotic anxiety – anxiety which is inexplicable by reference to the real uncertainties of life and requires the assumption that the anxiety-provoking object or situation has acquired an additional unconscious symbolic meaning. For instance, people who are, they say, frightened of heights are not in fact frightened of altitude *per se* (they can often fly in aeroplanes without anxiety) but are frightened lest the high building they are on will collapse or, more commonly, lest they may be overcome by a compulsion to throw themselves down to the ground – this wish-fear being the symbolic expression of a conflict about one's self-image. Does one wish to enjoy an elevated position above others, or does one wish to come down to earth and have one's feet on the ground?

In the preceding paragraphs I have been emphasizing the connections of anxiety with uncertainties about the future and therefore with such emotions as alertness, expectancy, hope, uneasiness, dread. All of these emotions hinge on the fact that in truth the future is uncertain, and that since it is uncertain an element of anxiety cannot but enter into our attitude towards it, notwithstanding our attempts to reduce this by plans for personal and social security or by reliance on ideologies such as science and religion which give us the illusion, the faith, that the future either is predictable or will, at least, continue to conform to some familiar and comprehensible pattern.

As a result of this emphasis on futurity I have so far under-played the connections between anxiety and immediate, press-ing emotions such as anguish and agony. Nor have I attempted to define (as I did in my book) the differences between anxiety on the one hand and fright, terror and shock on the other. And so far I have said nothing about anxiety attacks or dreams.

My reason for adopting this one-sided or lop-sided approach is that it does, I think, make it easier to understand two fundamental psychoanalytical concepts: signal-anxiety and separation-anxiety.

Now Freud, as I mentioned earlier, had at different times three different theories of anxiety. According to the first, anxiety was a manifestation, expression, transformation of libido; as a pre-senting symptom, it was the result of a disturbance in the patient's sexual life. If the patient engaged in excessive sexual activity and exhausted him- or herself, he or she developed neurasthenia; if the patient suffered (or enjoyed) excessive sex-ual stimulation but without appropriate orgastic discharge, he or she developed an anxiety-neurosis. Both neurasthenia and anxiety-neurosis were regarded as the *physiological* conse-quence of a disturbance in the patient's present sexual life; one being the result of a depletion of libido, the other of an excessive accumulation and damming up of it. Freud categorized these two syndromes together, calling them the 'actual neuroses', in contradistinction to the 'psychoneuroses', which he believed were due to disturbances in the patient's *past* sexual life – infantile sexual traumata and fantasies, the survival under repression of infantile sexual wishes.

Now one does on occasion encounter patients whose anxiety is rather obviously correlated with present or past disturbances in their sexual life. But the idea that anxiety is essentially transformed libido and that therefore all experiences of being anxious, whether awake or asleep, are expressions of repressed libidinal wishes, raises so many problems about the nature of libido – what sort of a thing or idea is it and what is the physiology of its transformability into anxiety? – that Freud, despite his strong attachment to the idea, was eventually forced to abandon it in favour of the purely psychological idea that anxiety is essentially a signal of impending danger.

However, before discussing signal-anxiety I must mention that Freud's original conviction that anxiety is transformed libido played an important part in his wish-fulfilment theory of dreams. Anxiety dreams are on the face of it rather obvious objections to the idea that all dreams are hallucinatory wish-fulfilments, but if anxiety is held to be essentially a form of libidinal discharge, then the occurrence of anxiety in a dream, so far from being an objection, becomes powerful evidence that a sexual wish is being expressed in it. So when, in the 1920s, Freud abandoned the theory of anxiety he had held in the 1890s when writing *The Interpretation of Dreams*, he removed one of the foundations of his own central theory. It is not clear to me whether Freud himself appreciated that he had done this (see my book *The Innocence of Dreams*, pp. 107–8).

Freud's conception of signal-anxiety is essentially an intro-verted version of the idea of anxiety as hyper-vigilance that I described earlier. Whereas normal extraverted anxiety is the response to some external stimulus or situation, the nature of which cannot as yet be assessed, signal-anxiety is the response of the ego to some threatening internal change. It is an alerting device which forewarns the ego of an impending threat to its equilibrium. The basic idea here is that the ego grows, not exclusively or even predominantly by unfolding and elaborating its potentialities, but, first, by repression of its infantile instincts (which then, hopefully, undergo symbolic displacements and sublimation) and, secondly, by internalization of parental auth-ority figures, who determine what is permitted and what is forbidden. The poor ego is thus at risk from two sources: from its own drives, which may overwhelm it, and from its internalized parental figures, its super-ego, which may punish it. Both may, it is imagined, annihilate it. It has, therefore, to become hyper-vigilant, alert to the possibility that it may be overwhelmed by its drives and its emotions or punished by its super-ego, and ready, ever ready, to protect its integrity from the onslaughts of these two hostile forces.

It does this by activating one or other of the various defences that constitute its repertoire of self-protective devices. In *Anxiety and Neurosis* I attempted to show that these defences are homologous to the basic adaptive responses used by animals (and man) when faced with external dangers – fight, flight and submission. For instance, obsessionals use fight, attack and mastery, while phobics and schizoids use flight and withdrawal, and hysterics use submission. If this idea is correct – and I still think there is something in it – the ego alerts itself and adapts itself to its external world and its internal reality in similar ways. Which is, I suppose, what one would expect.

Now, although I am not sure that I really subscribe to the rather gloomy view of human nature suggested by this account of the ego as perpetually hyper-vigilant in the face of instinctual and super-ego threats, it seems to me that it does fit obsessionality very well. So I shall now describe two dreams, one dreamt by an obsessional which actually symbolizes signal-anxiety, another dreamt by a man who was not obsessional and appeared to have a defective capacity for vigilance.

In the first dream, a coastal town received news that a tidal wave was approaching. The mayor of the town ordered alarm bells to be sounded and the inhabitants took all necessary precautions. The dreamer then woke up. This is hyper-vigilance with a vengeance. The defences are put into operation before the tidal wave becomes visible, and nothing in the dream gives any hint as to what the threatening wave might symbolize – whether it symbolizes his own impulses, his own capacity for rage or lust, perhaps, or the threat of being overwhelmed by what the jargon calls the 'bad, internal mother'.

In the second dream, the dreamer, a young man who had recently finished his National Service, imagined that he was falling into some complex machinery, was already caught up in it, and only woke up just as he was about to be dismembered. This was a recurrent nightmare from which he awoke several nights a week drenched in sweat. It meant nothing to him apart from the distress it was causing him, but when he and his therapist realized that the machinery was a conflation of a threshing machine and an electricity generating plant, both of which his father had owned, its meaning soon became apparent.

When he returned home after being demobbed, he discovered that his father had already organized a career for him without consulting him. He had accepted his father's plan without protest and had already begun training for it when the nightmares began. Here we have defective vigilance. In his waking life he had failed to appreciate that embarking on a career arranged without reference to his own wishes and aptitudes constituted a threat to his ego, or a threat to his identity, and in his nightmare he only woke up after he had got entangled in the machinery and become terrified.

Freud would have called this patient's terror 'primary anxiety' on the ground that signal-anxiety was a secondary formation. Its function was to ensure that another, elemental, catastrophic form of Angst, anguish or anxiety, that which accompanies dissolution of the ego, would never occur. (Incidentally, Freud's wish-fulfilment theory of dreams and his first theory of anxiety could be saved in this case by assuming that the young man had passive homosexual wishes towards his father which were gratified by his nightmares.)

Finally, I must say something about separation-anxiety, anxiety at the prospect or fact of being separated from someone felt to be necessary for one's survival. This fits simply into the schema I have been presenting since the person from whom one dreads separation is familiar and known, while the state of affairs to be confronted without one's protector is unfamiliar and uncertain. There is, however, more to be said than this.

First, separation-anxiety can be realistic and adaptive and is so in the case of infants and invalids, who are objectively dependent on the protective vigilance of their mother or nurse. The signs of distress displayed by infants threatened with separation fulfil the functions both of preparing the child to make an adaptive response and also, more importantly, of alerting the mother and heightening her viligance. To put this rather obvious point another way, during infancy and early childhood, when a child actually is incapable of surviving on its own and is, to use Piaget's term, heteronomous, separation-anxiety is the response to a threat that the mother–infant dyad, the primary identification between mother and infant, is at risk of being disrupted precociously, before the child is mature enough to be capable of functioning autonomously.

As Bowlby in particular has shown, this anxiety is realistic, since there is abundant evidence that premature separation of the young from their mothers can cause lasting damage, including damage to the capacity to develop healthy vigilance. H. S. Liddell compared the adult behaviour of sheep who had been prematurely separated from their mothers with that of their twins who had not. The separated sheep reacted feebly and dithered 'neurotically' when exposed to stress, unlike their twins who reacted energetically and vigorously. Rather similarly, adult humans who are, as the jargon has it, 'passively dependent' respond to stress not by vigilance and purposeful activity but by distress-signals designed to arouse the concern and vigilance of others.

Secondly, although separation-anxiety in infancy must be accounted normal, the fact that the human mother–infant relationship is so frequently permeated with ambivalence means that it tends to be compounded by another form of anxiety. Insofar as the infant becomes hostile towards its mother, it will be liable to anxiety lest its anger towards her will drive her away or destroy her. Insofar as it imagines or perceives that its mother is hostile, it will fear that she will abandon or destroy it. In either case the infant becomes liable to primary anxiety about its continued survival and will mobilize its defences. The fear of dissolution of the ego which Freud thought lay behind the need to develop signal-anxiety must derive, I think, from this infantile fear that the mother–infant relationship could become mutually destructive.

It seems to me that this primary anxiety, the dread that the ego, the self, is in danger of being destroyed utterly, which seems to lie at the back of so many neuroses, is the opposite of the 'oceanic feeling' described by Romain Rolland as the source of religious sentiments. In his *Civilization and Its Discontents* (1930), Freud interpreted this 'oceanic feeling' as a revival of the infant's experience at the breast before it has learnt to distinguish its ego from the outside world, itself from the other. Whereas the oceanic feeling recaptures and idealizes the sense of loving fusion with the breast, the dreaded primary anxiety would be experienced, it is imagined, if a mutually destructive collision occurred between self and other.

1987

John Bowlby, *Attachment and Loss*, vol. II: *Separation: Anxiety and Anger* (London: The Hogarth Press, 1973).

Sigmund Freud, 'On the Grounds for Detaching a Particular Syndrome from Neurasthenia under the Description "Anxiety Neurosis"' (1894) *Standard Edition*, vol. 3 (London: The Hogarth Press, 1962).

  'Sexuality in the Aetiology of the Neuroses', *SE*, vol. 13 (London: The Hogarth Press, 1962).

  'Inhibitions, Symptoms and Anxiety', *SE*, vol. 20 (London: The Hogarth Press, 1962).

H. S. Liddell, 'The Role of Vigilance in the Development of Animal Neurosis', in *Anxiety* ed. P. Hoch and J. Zubin (New York: Hafner, 1950).

Charles Rycroft, *A Critical Dictionary of Psychoanalysis* (London: Nelson, 1968; Harmondsworth: Penguin Books, 1972).

  Anxiety and Neurosis (London: Allen Lane, 1968; Harmondsworth: Penguin Books, 1970).

  The Innocence of Dreams (London: The Hogarth Press, 1979, 1991).

3

Where Is Psychoanalysis Going?

This was a contribution to a discussion on the future of psychotherapy, held in 1985 at the Royal Society of Medicine. Now,
five years later, there are only two points that I would like to add.
Object-relations theory is arousing greater interest in the United
States than one could have predicted then, and also my text
underestimates the extent to which Winnicott's and Klein's
versions of object-relations theory are incompatible; the discord
between them which was so painful and obvious when they were
alive still survives, alas, as ill-feeling between their followers.

There are, I think, several possible answers to the question
'where is psychoanalysis going?', since psychoanalysis is, of
course, not a single thing or object only capable of movement in
one direction, of only going up or down, forwards or backwards
or sideways, but a set of ideas, techniques and activities subject
to change, development, reformulation and reassessment, which
exists, not in a vacuum but in a social, intellectual, moral milieu
that is itself subject to change – and which has, indeed, changed
profoundly since 1896 when Freud first used the term 'psychoanalysis' to describe the form of psychotherapy he began
to develop after he abandoned hypnosis in favour of 'free
association'.

It is, then, more than ninety years since psychoanalysis began
to get going, and, incidentally, seventy-eight years since, following Freud's quarrel with Jung – or should it be Jung's quarrel
with Freud? – it underwent fission and started going in two
directions at once, and it became necessary for anyone wishing
to have a training analysis to decide in advance, and often on

grossly inadequate evidence, whether he was going to become a Freudian or a Jungian. I mention these two dates, 1896 and 1912, to draw attention to the fact that psychoanalysis began and suffered its first major split before most of us here were born, and to suggest that two of the several possible answers to the question 'Where is psychoanalysis going?' hinge quite simply upon the passage of time.

First, psychoanalysis, at least as Freud formulated and understood it, is moving out of the contemporary present into the historical past. Nowadays students who wish to know about the origins of psychoanalysis, about the genesis of Freud's ideas, about the intellectual and social matrix out of which psychoanalysis arose, about the personal and philosophical incompatibilities that resulted in the Freud–Jung split, are no longer dependent on the obviously partisan accounts left by Freud and Jung and their loyal and devoted disciples, but can instead turn to the work of professional historians and biographers, who are concerned not with the dissemination of myths and legends about idealized heroes, but with setting the record straight, with unearthing lost or hidden documentary evidence, and with putting ideas and people into their historical and social context.

Secondly, now that the Founding Fathers and their immediate successors and disciples are passing into history, psychoanalysis is beginning to extricate itself from its earlier compulsion to refight the battles of yesteryear and from the tendency to form cliques and schools dependent upon a charismatic leader, and a greater broad-mindedness, tolerance and eclecticism seems to be in the air. For instance, although in Britain the two leading psychoanalytical institutes still formally differentiate themselves as Freudian and Jungian, one hears of seminars on Jung organized by the Freudian institute, of therapeutic institutions where Jungians and Freudians work happily together, so far as one can tell, of Freud–Jung discussion groups, and even of attempts to integrate the work of Jung with that of two latter-day Freudians, Klein and Winnicott. Furthermore, there are now associations, centres, guilds, clinics and foundations where generic, unlabelled pyschotherapy is taught, though most of the training is in fact conducted by Freudian and Jungian analysts. All this collaboration, which would have been inconceivable twenty years ago, strongly suggests that the psychoanalytical movements are abandoning their exclusiveness and renouncing their claims that they are upholders of the only true psychodynamic theory and that all other psychotherapeutic theories are either dangerous heresies or ineffectual dilutions. An ecumenical spirit seems to be around here as elsewhere, and here as elsewhere it is being purchased at the price of a certain loss of intellectual rigour.

So far I have spoken as though there were only two psychodynamic schools of thought embraceable under the term 'psychoanalysis' – the Freudian and the Jungian – but this is, of course, not so. In Britain, object-relations theory, as propounded in different ways by Klein, Winnicott, Fairbairn and Bowlby, has become increasingly influential and the path being laid out by object-theorists must, I think and hope, be where psychoanalysis is going.

Now, although object-relations theorists claim to be Freudian, and indeed certainly are inasmuch as they believe in unconscious mental processes, in fantasy, in trasference, and in the therapeutic value of free association and symbolic interpretation, they – or should I say we? – hold that the heart of the matter lies not, as Freud thought, in the pursuit of pleasure and in the generation, control and discharge of instinctual tensions, but in the individual's relations to his objects, that is, in the history of his attachments to, separations from, and losses of, loving and loved people from infancy onwards.

This shift in interest from questions of libidinal tension and psychic economy on to relations with objects, that is people, is, I believe, humanizing psychoanalysis. By this I mean several things. First, it compels analysts to recognize that they relate to their patients, albeit in a most peculiar way, and do not as an outsider just observe their mental processes. Secondly, metaphors derived from physics and neuro-anatomy (the cathexes, counter-cathexes and hypercathexes, the quanta of psychic energy being transferred from one structure within the psychic apparatus to another), impersonal metaphors which implied that psychoanalysis was the same kind of science or discipline as

physics and chemistry and that the laws of causation appropriate to the natural sciences applied equally to human behaviour –
such metaphors are being replaced by human, humanist metaphors which allow that human beings are agents who make
choices and decisions, who can act sincerely or insincerely, truly
or falsely, who generate meaning whenever they act and
attribute meaning to whatever they perceive, and whose inner
world is populated by images of past and present figures who are
or have been loved, hated or feared.

Thirdly, as a result of this shift it has become possible to talk
about internal mental states and activities in the same language
as we all use to talk about relations between people, thereby
making dialogue and interaction between analysts and other
professional groups concerned with human behaviour and its
meaning easier and more fruitful. In the early days of psychoanalysis much was written about the enormous and indispensable contribution that psychoanalysis could make to
anthropology, to history, to the social sciences, to aesthetics, but
the language in which psychoanalytical ideas were formulated
was such as to render them opaque to the very people who, it was
averred, most needed to be enlightened by them. Nor was much
said about the possibility that psychoanalysis might have much
to learn from other disciplines.

However, the climate is, I think, changing. I doubt, for
instance, whether many analysts in practice still follow Ernest
Jones in insisting that the only true symbols are those used by
dreamers constructing a disguised hallucinatory fulfilment of a
repressed wish, and that anthropologists and linguists are in
grievous error when they use the word 'symbol' to refer to
words, badges, emblems and rituals – a piece of restrictive word-
defining which must have effectively blocked communication
between analysts and anthropologists for some forty years. And
I doubt whether I am – indeed, I know that I am not – the only
analyst who uses the concept of 'rite de passage' to help patients
over the hurdle from adolescence to adulthood, or uses Gregory
Bateson's double-bind hypothesis to elucidate the tangles into
which spouses, and parents and children, get themselves.

Psychoanalysis, and in particular object-relations theory, is beginning to speak a less esoteric language, is beginning to talk about human nature in terms of relationships between people rather than in terms of movements of libido within isolated psychic apparatuses, and by so doing is being enabled both to communicate its insights better to others – witness the remarkable influence of Winnicott's writings on social workers and the caring, counselling professions generally – and to allow itself to be influenced by other disciplines. So another answer to the question 'Where is psychoanalysis going?' is that it is coming out of the closet, is recovering from its agoraphobia, which in the early days *may* have been based on an objective perception of external reality, and is entering the marketplace where it can influence, and allow itself to be influenced by, group therapists, family therapists, existential therapists, cognitive psychologists and others.

Although this diffusion of psychoanalytical ideas is, for obvious practical reasons, to be welcomed, it is, I think, just possible that something is at the same time being lost. Perhaps there is something valuable, private but inherently esoteric about the long-term intensive psychoanalytical encounter which eludes the contemporary vogue for short-term relationship-orientated psychotherapies; and perhaps research into such obscurities as the genesis of self-awareness and symbolic thinking, the relationship of the self to its self, its body, its sexuality, requires greater intensity of contact and greater intellectual rigour than the contemporary psychotherapies can afford.

1985

Gregory Bateson *et al.*, 'Towards a Theory of Schizophrenia', in *Steps to an Ecology of the Mind* (St Albans: Paladin, 1973).

John Bowlby, *Attachment and Loss*, 3 vols (London: The Hogarth Press, 1969, 1973, 1980).

Vincent Brome, *Jung: Man and Myth* (London: Macmillan, 1978).

Ronald W. Clark, *Freud: The Man and the Cause* (London: Jonathan Cape and Weidenfeld & Nicolson, 1980).

W. R. D. Fairbairn, *Psychoanalytic Studies of the Personality* (London: Tavistock, 1952).

Melanie Klein, *Contributions to Psychoanalysis* (London: The Hogarth Press, 1948).

Charles Rycroft, 'Causes and Meaning', in *Psychoanalysis Observed* (London: Constable, 1966).
  'Is Freudian Symbolism a Myth?' in *Symbols and Sentiments*, ed. Ioan Lewis (London: Academic Press, 1977).
Roy Schafer, *A New Language for Psychoanalysis* (New Haven and London: Yale University Press, 1976).
Frank J. Sulloway, *Freud, Biologist of the Mind* (London: Burnett Books and André Deutsch, 1979).
D. W. Winnicott, *Collected Papers* (London: Tavistock, 1958).

4

Why Psychiatry Is an Intrinsically Odd Profession

I must confess that I have no recollection of writing this piece, but I am fairly certain that I must have written it in an attempt to give a rational, serious, abstract formulation of an idea that I used to float, in a somewhat light-hearted way, during the 1960s. This was that the invention of terms like 'trick-cycling' and 'head-shrinking' to describe the activities of psychiatrists and psychoanalysts revealed a popular insight into the fact that psychiatry and psychoanalysis are not quite what they seem and claim to be; there is some peculiar discrepancy between the flag under which psychiatrists and analysts sail and the activities in which they engage.

The aim of this note is to propose that the psychiatrist's social function is not, as most psychiatrists and their patients believe, to treat mental illnesses. Instead it is to be an expert in dealing with those aspects of human behaviour which do not fit into commonly used categories; to be expert, in other words, in dealing with behaviour which seems strange, odd, peculiar and anomalous to the society which employs these categories and accords them status. This idea, which occurred to me while reading Mary Douglas's *Purity and Danger* (1966), is based on the following three assumptions:

1. All societies, and indeed all individuals taken singly too, attempt to impose order on the universe by establishing categories into which, in theory, all phenomena can be fitted.

2. These prevailing categories do not, in fact, work, and there always remains a range of phenomena which cannot be fitted into them.

3. Phenomena which resist categorization evoke peculiar emotional reactions, varying from anxiety and disgust to fascination and awe, and are felt to be in some strange way 'taboo', 'unclean' or 'sacred'.

To give two examples of what I mean. Our society categorizes objects as either animate or inanimate, but, since people and animals die, there exist corpses, which don't fit into this division, since they were once alive but now aren't. If we try to regard them as inanimate things, we are defeated by the fact that their posture and facial expression still appear to have meaning; if we try to regard them as animate creatures we are defeated by the fact that they are inert and unresponsive. As a result, superstitions, uncanny feelings and rituals surround our attitude to corpses. Even the skeletons of the long dead evoke such reactions. Doctors are trained to overcome these uncanny feelings by spending a large part of their student days dissecting corpses, in the course of which they become familiar with the body as an inanimate object and learn the art of being able to treat living ones as though they were machines. Even the most hardened, however, refrain from inspecting human bones in public places or performing dissections outside the special sacred places allocated to them for engaging in their professional initiation rites.

Secondly, we make a clear distinction between what is our self and what is not our self, but what about faeces, nail-parings and hair-clippings? One moment they are part of ourselves, the next moment they aren't, and as a result they form the subject of numerous taboos and rituals, only some of which can be justified on hygienic grounds. They also play a remarkably important part in the fantasy life of neurotics and children and the delusions of psychotics, i.e. of those who have yet to learn or failed to learn society's categories.

Similarly with behaviour, including utterances. When people talk about themselves, we commonly assume that they are either telling the truth or telling lies, but there are people who say things about themselves which are neither. There are, for instance, people who assert with obvious sincerity that they are miserable sinners who have committed the most dreadful crimes, but who quite patently haven't; and there are other people who assert with equal sincerity that they are someone who in fact they are not and who, to confound matters further, do not expect anyone to treat them as though they were the person they assert themselves to be. I am, of course, referring to 'insane' people who are treated and cared for by psychiatrists, and who, until recently at least, were the objects of general fear and superstition, segregated from the rest of the population in special prison-like institutions – partly for their own sakes, but partly to protect others from contamination.

In psychiatric jargon such people are deluded, a delusion being an idea which is false but is not a lie. But this descriptive label – and the diagnosis, depressive psychosis or schizophrenia, of which it forms a part – really constitutes no more than a category within which to include the uncategorizable, incomprehensible fact that people can sincerely utter statements about themselves which are neither truths nor lies, or even simple errors. It offers no sort of explanation of what psychotic people mean when they say things that are neither true nor deliberately untrue. In fact, psychiatrists differ among themselves about the kind of answer they give to the question 'What do delusional statements mean?' One group, the so-called organic school of psychiatry, asserts that they are in fact meaningless, being merely by-products of some metabolic or cerebral disorder. The other, the psychodynamic school, believes that they can be given meaning if only one can crack the code in which they have been formulated.

Another assumption we generally make is that people are either physically well or suffering from some, in principle, definable diagnosable physical illness. But unfortunately for our peace of mind, there exist people who claim – and can indeed demonstrate – that their bodies don't work properly but who suffer from no known physical illness. Their physical disabilities, if accepted as such, would make nonsense of everything we know about anatomy and physiology. Most ordinary doctors tend to be impatient with such people, whom they suspect of being impostors who are trying to have them on, but psychiatrists call them hysterics and regard them as legitimate patients. Psychoanalysis, indeed, owes its origin to the discovery made by

Freud and Breuer in the 1890s that hysterical physical symptoms have psychological meaning and can be interpreted as reactions to former psychological events. In other words, they explained a previously entirely mysterious group of physical symptoms by recategorizing them, or rather by inventing a new category, that of psychogenic physical symptoms unaccompanied by physical pathology, into which they could be placed. But such is the rigidity of society's habitual categories that even today, nearly a century later, it is still difficult either to explain or understand this category or to see how to fit it into our conception of the natural order of things.

Lastly, deeply imbedded in our culture and language is the assumption that we consist of two bits, a body and a mind, but again there are people whose lives demonstrate that this distinction doesn't always hold. Such people develop true physical illnesses in response to mental stress and distress, thereby making nonsense both of medicine as a branch of the physical sciences and of many varieties of psychology and theology. Such people, or rather their illnesses, can only be explained by inventing a new category, psychosomatic illness, to include illnesses which cannot be allocated to either the body or the mind, and which indeed call into question the validity of the distinction.

It would seem, therefore, that the role of psychiatrists in society is that of dealing with people whose behaviour infringes three laws or rules which society generally assumes to be valid and which are deeply imbedded in its linguistic habits and its social conventions, viz. that when people say things about themselves they are either telling the truth or telling lies, that people are either physically well or suffering from a physical illness localizable in some particular part of the body, and that all our experiences can be referred to one or other of two putative bits, the body or the mind. It would seem too, to judge by the historical and anthropological evidence, that most societies and cultures invent a class of people, priests, shamans, witch-doctors, and so forth, whose job it is to remain undismayed by those phenomena which do not fit into the category-systems used by the culture at large and who claim to have some expertise in dealing with them. Many of the ambiguities and peculiarities of contemporary psychiatry derive from the fact that in a scientific age like our own, experts in the anomalous have to claim to be scientists and to derive their prestige and respectability from membership of a scientific profession. Even in Europe this has not always been so; until the eighteenth century the care of the insane was often the task of the clergy; and it was the philosophers, not the doctors, who claimed to be able to explain insanity.

c. 1969

5

Model and Metaphor in Psychology

This talk opened a discussion on model and metaphor in psychology held in London on 7 May 1969, organized by the Canadian Broadcasting Corporation and, presumably, later broadcast in Canada. Although I wrote and delivered it over twenty years ago, the points it makes are as important now as they were then. It seems to me that in psychoanalysis, and probably in other disciplines, controversies are as often about the choice of metaphor on which theory should be based as they are disagreements on questions of fact. For instance, ego-psychologists still remain loyal to Freud's idea that mental activity was best conceptualized as the activity of a fictive, space-occupying 'psychic apparatus', while object-relations theorists, both Winnicottian and Kleinian, prefer to personify psychic structures and to conceive of an 'inner world' inhabited by person-like 'internal objects'.

I should like to open by asserting dogmatically that we *inevitably* use metaphor when talking about mental activity. Thoughts and feelings, the raw material of psychology, or at least of subjective psychologies such as psychoanalysis, are experiences which people have, not phenomena which people observe, but when we try to describe them we are compelled to use analogies derived from phenomena which we do observe. We talk of our thoughts *flowing* freely or otherwise, of our *seeing* the *point* of an argument or failing to do so; we attribute *warmth* to our affectionate emotions and *coldness* to hate; at every turn we are compelled to draw on our knowledge of the physical world in order to describe our subjective experiences. And yet subjective experiences lack many of the attributes of the physical world which the language of the natural sciences has been constructed to describe and explain. In particular, they lack location in space, they lack size, shape and weight. Perhaps, indeed, the only property they share with material phenomena is duration in time. They last for a certain length of time, they can be arranged serially and, perhaps, synchronously, they display continuity, discontinuity and recurrence.

This anomalous character of psychology is commonly dealt with both in ordinary language and in scientific writing by recourse to a metaphorical fiction. We postulate a *mind*, which is imagined to be a space inside which mental activity occurs. This mind is further imagined as an organ, so that we conceive ourselves as having in addition to arms, legs, a heart and brain, another organ, a mind, which resembles the others in having functions, those of thinking and being conscious. Nowadays we come very near to taking this anatomical metaphor literally by asserting that this mind has some sort of intrinsic connection with the brain, an assumption which involves us in all sorts of puzzling problems about mind–body relationships and the connection between psychological and neurological phenomena. As a result of embarking on this anatomical metaphor, we reach a position in which we can construct theories about the experiences of whole persons *as though* they were the functions of an organ possessed by persons. This enables us to get the subjective, private and invisible into the realm of the objective, public and visible. The metaphorical device we have used is synecdoche, albeit of a curious kind, which enables us to theorize about the experiences of whole persons by describing them as though they were the functions of a fictitious part.

The procedure of talking about psychology as though it were the study of an anatomical organ is clearly exemplified by the early history of psychoanalysis. Freud started life as an anatomist and neurologist, and his earliest formulations were a conscious, deliberate attempt to construct a psychology which would be neurologically based. The mind was called a psychic apparatus, 'ideas' were conceived to be like nerve cells with associative fibres linking them, and emotions, 'affects', were thought of as like charges of electrical energy which could flow from one idea to another or could be discharged in action. Even later, when Freud abandoned as hopeless the attempt to construct a neurological psychology and turned to the formation of a pure, autonomous psychology, he still thought anatomically and drew diagrams of the psychic apparatus on which various structures, notably an ego, an id, and a super-ego, were located. This procedure enabled him to construct a *model* of the mind which enabled him to use spatial metaphors to describe temporally related phenomena. Differences in *quality* between mental processes, such as whether they were conscious or unconscious, primitive or sophisticated, rational or phantastic, objective or moralistic, were explained by locating them in different positions in the psychic apparatus.

The anatomical, neurological metaphor is still very much alive in psychoanalysis, and there must be many people today who believe that they really do have an ego, an id and a super-ego, and who fail to realize that to Freud they were only fictions which he felt were necessary to bring scientific order into psychology. Recent developments in psychoanalysis suggest, however, that the anatomical model may be giving way to a new one. The impersonal, pseudo-anatomical structures of the psychic apparatus are being repersonified, and mental processes which Freud would have located in the super-ego are being explained in terms of what are called 'internal objects' – the spatial metaphor is being retained – such as 'internal fathers' and 'internal mothers', phantoms conceived to inhabit the mind and to exert a dynamic effect on the subject as though they were people with an autonomous life of their own. One hears talk, too, of internal communication, internal relationships, sometimes even internal communities. What seems to be happening is that the underlying model and metaphor is changing and the person is being thought of, not as someone who possesses a mind, but as a *social system* consisting of the person's self and representatives, or rather representations of his past and present objects. The medical, anatomical, neurological model is being abandoned and replaced by a sociological model.

This fact exemplifies the last point I want to make. The models and metaphors used by psychology are borrowed from other sciences, the particular science chosen depending on the individual biography of the particular theorist or on its social prestige and dominance during any particular historical period. In the Middle Ages psychology, insofar as it existed, borrowed from theology; what we now call mental illness was due to sin or demoniacal possession, and recovery from mental illness was due to God's mercy or to exorcism. From, say, 1850 to 1950, psychologies, whether clinical or academic, psychoanalytical or behaviouristic, all used models derived from the natural sciences. Of recent years there seems to be an attempt, not as yet fully established, to use models derived from sociology, linguistics, semantics and cybernetics. It seems that our view of man is profoundly and inescapably affected by our views of nature and of society. Ideas derived from our study of the external world reflect back on our view of ourselves, giving us changing models and metaphors with which to describe ourselves. John Cohen starts his book *Humanistic Psychology* (1958) with a chapter called 'The Difficulty of Making the First Step', in which he lists the following sciences as having provided models for psychology: physics, chemistry, geology (layers of the mind), mathematics, embryology (stages of libidinal development), epidemiology – and he could now add linguistics, sociology and semantics. He also uses as his epigraph to this book a pregnant if obscure quotation from Kafka: 'Psychology is the description of the reflection of the terrestrial world on the heavenly plane.'

1969

FREUD, FELLOWS AND CRITICS

6

Why Freud and Jung Could Never Agree

This is a slightly shortened version of my review of Robert
S. Steele's *Freud and Jung: Conflicts of Interpretation*. It is, I
think, worth preserving (and Steele's book itself is still worth
reading) since it states in a nutshell the temperamental, cultural
and philosophical reasons why Freud and Jung could never in a
thousand years have agreed with one another.

In addressing himself to the differences between the Freudian
and Jungian systems of thought, Robert Steele argues that these
do not, as is commonly believed, hinge on the fact that Freud was
scientific and Jung unscientific, but on the fact that they had
profoundly different visions of reality and therefore constructed
radically different psychologies.*
    Steele is, if I understand him rightly, concerned not to take
sides in the controversies between Jung and Freud, and between
Jungians and Freudians, but rather to demonstrate that hermeneutics, the art or science of interpretation, enables one to
take up a detached vantage point, from which it can be seen that
both have illuminated man's understanding of himself and have
thereby added to man's sense of his own meaning.
    As Dr Steele points out, hermeneutics began as the art of
interpreting religious texts which were believed to be inspired,
and even in the contemporary secular version he practises it
presumes that a real dialogue takes place between the hermeneut
and the texts he is interpreting. As a result, Dr Steele can claim

* Robert S. Steele, *Freud and Jung: Conflicts of Interpretation* (London:
Routledge & Kegan Paul, 1982).

that his book is a report on the dialogue that has taken place
between himself and Freud and Jung, during which they told him
more than they knew they were telling when they wrote the texts
to which Dr Steele has applied himself – and with which he has,
in his own terms, been in textual dialogue. I must confess to
feeling most unhappy about all this and inhibited by the thought
that as Steele's reviewer I may unwittingly overstep the conven-
tion by which a reviewer merely reports on the book he is
reviewing.

It is clear, however, that Freud and Jung are ideal subjects for
the practice of hermeneutics. They both constructed psychologies based on the assumption that human behaviour, thought
and feelings can be interpreted and given meanings more than
and other than the individual himself appreciates. They both
based their psychologies on their own self-analyses, during
which, so they claimed, they discovered general truths about
human nature by interpreting their own dreams, imaginings and
childhood recollections; as a result of which their private visions
and versions of themselves and their public theories about
human nature became inextricably intertwined. And, during
their few years of cooperation, they attempted, with remarkable
lack of success, to enter into a meaningful dialogue with one
another.

Since Freud and Jung were both prolific writers, and since,
furthermore, their self-analyses are well documented and their
private letters to one another have been published, Dr Steele has
had no lack of material on which to practise his hermeneutic arts
and the judgments he makes are well supported by evidence.

In Dr Steele's view Freudian and Jungian theory are both
hermeneutic systems which enable existence to be given form
and meaning by constructing coherent narratives out of the
seemingly haphazard details of individual lives. Jung recognized
this and made no claim to be a natural scientist, but Freud
always insisted that he was one and that psychoanalysis was the
same sort of science as physics and chemistry, always claiming
that the interpretations he made of, for instance, dreams and
symptoms were ideas already present, albeit unconsciously, in
the mind. As a result he maintained that the interpretations he

made after having or being told a dream were formulations in words of non-verbal unconscious ideas that had been present before the dream and had caused it. This is precisely the point I made in the essay 'Causes and Meaning' printed in *Psychoanalysis Observed* (1966) and which Thomas Szasz had made at greater length in *The Myth of Mental Illness* (1961).

Dr Steele also believes that for two reasons Freud and Jung could never have come to an agreement. First, their dogmatic temperaments made them incapable of creative dialogue with one another. 'Their letters do not reveal two men with great analytic insight helping each other to explore their own psychic depths or two great minds continually grappling with the riddles of human nature [but] two intelligent people trying to stay on the good side of one another, heaping abuse on their enemies, . . . and, sadly, avoiding any revelations to one another that they did not have to make.'

Second, their interpretative systems were based on irreconcilable philosophical premises. Freud remained loyal all his life to the scientific positivism he had absorbed while a student and believed that in psychoanalysis he had discovered a method for observing mental processes objectively, while Jung built on a neo-platonist thread that had been part of his family's Christian theological tradition and believed that ideas were the only true realities. Freud and Jung were, it seems, like the two angry fishwives abusing one another across the street who inspired Sydney Smith's punning joke: Those two will never agree: they are arguing from different premises.

1982

7

A Passionate Friendship – Freud and Fliess

This review of Jeffrey Masson's edition of the letters of Freud and Fliess* links what has been called 'Freud's creative illness' with the origins of psychoanalysis.

In December 1936 Reinhold Stahl, a Berlin bookseller, sold to Princess Marie Bonaparte, Princess George of Greece and Denmark, friend and pupil of Sigmund Freud, a set of documents he had acquired from the widow of Wilhelm Fliess (1858–1928), who in his day had been a successful ear, nose and throat specialist in Berlin and a well-known writer of speculative works about the relationship between the nose and the sexual organs and the part played in man's destiny by what are now called biorhythms.

These documents consisted of 270 letters from Freud to Fliess, fourteen enclosures (now known as drafts A–N) in which Freud had reported on his attempts to formulate a general psychological theory of the neuroses, and two notebooks which contained the 40,000-word manuscript of an untitled work (now known as 'Project for a Scientific Psychology'), in which Freud had attempted 'to furnish a psychology that shall be a natural science', that is, one in which 'psychical processes' were envisaged as 'quantitatively determinate states of specifiable material particles', viz. neurones (nerve cells).

Not surprisingly, Marie Bonaparte immediately informed Freud of her purchase. In his reply Freud told her that he did not

---

* *The Complete Letters of Sigmund Freud to Wilhelm Fliess 1887–1904* (Cambridge, Mass.: Harvard University Press, 1985).

have Fliess's letters to himself – 'I do not know to this day whether I destroyed them, or only hid them ingeniously' – offered to contribute to the expense she had incurred, and stated roundly: 'I do not want any of them to become known to so-called posterity.'

In March 1937 Marie Bonaparte took the documents to Vienna and showed them to Freud, who must, I think, have reread them, since he is on record as knowing which letters were missing and as remarking of one that it was 'very important'. He gave Marie Bonaparte permission to read them herself but tried to persuade her to destroy them. She refused and instead deposited them in the Rothschild Bank in Vienna, from which, after the Anschluss in March 1938, she removed them, using her trebly royal status to get round the Gestapo. From Vienna the documents went to Paris, where, in February 1941, Marie Bonaparte deposited them with the Danish Legation. They remained there until after the end of the war and were then shipped to London (where Sigmund Freud had died and Anna Freud was now living) 'wrapped in waterproof and buoyant material to give them a chance of survival' if the ship struck a mine.

At some date in the late 1940s Marie Bonaparte gave the letters to Anna Freud, who allowed Ernest Jones access to them while he was writing his Life of her father; and in 1964 she gave transcripts of them to Max Schur, who had been Freud's personal physician. His use of them to write a paper demonstrating that Freud's Irma dream, 'the Specimen Dream of Psycho-Analysis', had obvious connections with a dramatic and unedifying event in Freud's practice, to which he had *not* referred in his own analysis of it, gave rise to the idea that the complete Fliess letters might contain sensational details that would seriously dent Freud's image and might necessitate radical revision of the early history of psychoanalysis. In 1980 Anna Freud donated the letters to the Library of Congress, where they remain restricted from public view.

Meanwhile Anna Freud had published a selection of them. In 1950 *Aus den Anfängen der Psychoanalyse*, edited by Marie Bonaparte, Anna Freud and Ernst Kris, was published in

London, and an English translation, *The Origins of Psycho-Analysis*, appeared in 1954. This work includes all the drafts, the 'Project', but only 168 of the 270 letters – and of the 168 letters included, over 120 have suffered excisions, many of them trivial but some of them not.

To complicate matters further, a selection of the selection was included in Volume I of the *Standard Edition of the Complete Psychological Works of Sigmund Freud* (1966). Translated and edited by James Strachey, this further selection was made with the 'serious student' of psychoanalysis solely in mind. It contains thirty letters, all except one of the drafts, and the 'Project', and its numerous footnotes are concerned exclusively with establishing connections between theoretical ideas advanced in the letters and those developed at length in Freud's published and mostly later writings.

The Complete Letters of Sigmund Freud to Wilhelm Fliess: 1887-1904, translated and edited by Jeffrey Moussaieff Masson, is designed to complement and supplement these two earlier selections but not, I think, to supplant them. Not only does Masson in his own Introduction say that Ernst Kris's Introduction to the *Origins* is 'a milestone in the history of psycho-analysis, still unmatched today' and refer to James Strachey's 'improved translation and excellent notes', but he has also adopted a deliberate policy of not mentioning in his footnotes information that can be got from Kris's and Strachey's introductions and notes.

In my annotation I have attempted not to elaborate on the obvious, or to cite information that the reader can easily obtain (for example, by consulting Ernest Jones's three volume biography of Freud). For this reason I have frequently not reproduced material that is available in Ernst Kris's notes to the earlier edition of the letters, but have simply referred the reader to that edition. Nor have I duplicated Strachey's labors.

The 'Project' is not included in the *Complete Letters*.

Although this policy decision of Masson's reveals a becoming and perhaps surprising modesty, it has had the effect of making the *Complete Letters* a book that cannot be read on its own. Much of it will be incomprehensible to readers who have not got

a copy of the *Origins* to refer to, and its main interest derives
from the fact that it reveals precisely what in 1950 Anna Freud,
Marie Bonaparte and Ernst Kris saw fit, or felt entitled, not to
include in their selection.

However, if one refers back, as the present reviewer has had
to, to the Editors' Note to the *Origins*, one discovers that Anna
Freud and Ernst Kris – Marie Bonaparte seems not to have taken
part in the selection – were more concerned with what they were
entitled to publish than with what they were entitled to leave
out.

The selection was made on the principle of making public everything
relating to the writer's scientific work and scientific interests and
everything bearing on the social and political conditions in which
psycho-analysis originated; and of omitting or abbreviating everything
publication of which would be inconsistent with professional or personal confidence . . . The author of the material in this volume would
not have consented to the publication of any of it. It was Freud's habit to
destroy all notes and preliminary drafts as soon as they had served their
purpose, to publish nothing incomplete or unfinished, and to publish
material of a personal nature only when it was essential for the purpose
of demonstrating unconscious connections. These letters were brought
to light by chance, and the editors feel justified in publishing them in
spite of the hesitation which respect for the author's attitude in the
matter inevitably imposes.

In assessing Anna Freud's and Ernst Kris's editorial policy, it
has to be remembered that in the 1950s discretion and reticence
were still accounted virtues and, furthermore, that children and
relatives of both Freud and Fliess were still alive and active in
the psychoanalytical movement. Not only was Anna Freud the
daughter of Sigmund Freud, she was actually born during the
period when the letters were being written, and the *Complete
Letters* contain numerous references to her mother's health
while she was carrying her, to her birth, infancy and childhood,
and to the activities and illnesses of her elder brothers and sisters.
And although these references throw a pleasing light on Freud as
a husband and father, they have no bearing on the development
of his ideas, and one can appreciate why so many of them were
not included in a selection of letters which was designed to throw
light on *The Origins of Psycho-Analysis*.

Not only was Anna Freud the daughter of Sigmund Freud, the other selector, Ernst Kris, was married to a niece of Fliess's wife. He must also, I think, have been an acquaintance if not a friend of Robert Fliess, Wilhelm's son (and therefore a first cousin of his (Kris's) wife), who became a psychoanalyst. Several passages in the *Complete Letters* which do not appear in the *Origins* refer to Kris's father-in-law, Oscar Rie, and do so in an unpleasant, condescending way. Rie, it seems, was sceptical of both Freud's and Fliess's ideas, Fliess was contemptuous of Rie's rigidity, and Freud, during the period of his infatuation with Fliess, buttered him up by being nasty about Rie. As Rie was one of Freud's best and most longstanding friends, and paediatrician to Freud's children and, later, grandchildren, one can again appreciate why these passages were not included in the selection published in 1950.

Publication of the complete letters in 1950 would in fact have caused considerable embarrassment and distress among the editors' relatives, friends and colleagues, and one can understand why it was only in 1980, when Anna Freud was in her mid-eighties and had become one of the last survivors of the generation that had personal memories of and attachments to her father, to Fliess, and to their milieu in the 1890s, that, after considerable persuasion, she gave Jeffrey Moussaieff Masson access to the Fliess letters and permission to prepare a new, complete edition.

Although the editors of the *Origins* may well have been entirely justified in having been as discreet and selective as they were in 1950, Anna Freud and her circle must have appreciated that curiosity, which could not be dismissed as prurience, would eventually be aroused by every detail of Freud's life and would eventually have to be satisfied. But they seem to have wished to postpone the day as long as possible and to have adopted a policy towards Freud's papers which did, indeed, preserve all the evidence for posterity but nonetheless conveyed the impression that secrets, scandals and sensational details were being withheld. The Fliess letters were preserved, when Anna Freud could, I imagine, have destroyed them had she wished, but researchers were denied access to them, and other collections of Freud's correspondence were acquired, often by purchase, and placed in the Library of Congress, but with embargoes on them until well into the twenty-first century.

But as Freud claimed that he had made many of his revolutionary discoveries about sexuality and neurosis during the course of his own, unique self-analysis, and as the *Origins*, and also Chapter XIII of Vol. I of Jones's *Life*, had revealed that this self-analysis had been part and parcel of his relationship with Fliess, anyone wishing to check, question or challenge the validity and success of Freud's psychoanalysis of himself was bound to wish for access to the *Complete Letters*. And now we have them.

The first thing to be said about them is that they confirm to the hilt Jones's statements that Freud's relationship with Fliess was 'the only really extraordinary experience in Freud's life', that it was 'a passionate friendship for someone his inferior', in which for several years he subordinated his judgment and opinions to those of Fliess, and that he liberated himself from his thraldom by his self-analysis. For years Freud seems to have accepted uncritically every idea of Fliess's, however fanciful, to have deferred to him on every point, to have accepted his advice without demur, to have pined for his company – and then quite suddenly, in the letter which Freud in March 1937 declared was 'very important', he suddenly finds his own voice. He points out that he and Fliess have 'drawn apart to some extent', observes that Fliess's recent remark that 'the reader of thoughts merely reads his own thoughts into other people' constituted a complete devaluation of his work, and, in passages which are not in the *Origins*, accuses Fliess of uncharitableness towards mutual friends (Rie, Breuer) and of contempt for friendship between men. 'I do not share your contempt for friendship between men, probably because I am to a high degree party to it. In my life, as you know, woman has never replaced the comrade, the friend.'

This letter marks, I think, the end of the affair, and also of what Henri F. Ellenberger called Freud's 'creative illness'. In Ellenberger's words,

A creative illness succeeds a period of intense preoccupation with an idea and search for a certain truth. It is a polymorphous condition that can take the shape of depression, neurosis, psychosomatic ailments, or even psychosis. Whatever the symptoms, they are felt as painful if not agonizing, by the subject, with alternating periods of alleviation and worsening. Throughout the illness the subject never loses the thread of his dominating preoccupation. It is often compatible with normal, professional and family life. But even if he keeps to his social activities, he is almost entirely absorbed with himself. He suffers from feelings of utter isolation, even when he has a mentor who guides him through the ordeal. The termination is often rapid and marked by a phase of exhilaration. The subject emerges from his ordeal with a permanent transformation and the conviction that he has discovered a great truth or a new spiritual world.

Readers of the *Complete Letters* will discover that Freud went through just such a creative illness and that the insights he acquired into the meaning of dreams and symptoms, the Oedipus complex, the importance of fantasy, marked stages in his recovery.

Some of the consequences of Freud's long thraldom to Fliess, who proved a reluctant, unreliable mentor, were absurd and trivial; others were more fateful. Freud seems to have seriously believed for a while that his son Martin, born in 1889, wrote poetry and had nose-bleeds under the influence of his twenty-eight-day feminine bio-rhythm, which can have done no one any harm, but his faith in Fliess's theories about the nose and sexuality led to serious trouble.

Freud and Fliess both suffered from migraine and what was, I presume, chronic sinusitis. Fliess twice operated on Freud's nose, without either benefit or harm, Fliess's nose was operated on twice by some third party, again without benefit, but despite this lack of evidence for the efficacy of nasal psychosurgery, in 1895 Freud persuaded Fliess to operate on the nose of one of his (Freud's) neurotic patients, Emma Eckstein. Fliess inadvertently left half a metre of gauze in Emma Eckstein's nose, as a result of which she had numerous post-operative haemorrhages and nearly died. Freud, however, exonerated Fliess completely, denied that he had been in any way negligent, and eventually persuaded himself that Eckstein's bleeding had been hysterical, the expression of a longing for love. This incident was described by Max Schur in 1966 in his paper on the Specimen Dream of Psychoanalysis, and more recently, and in greater detail, by

Masson in Chapter II of his *The Assault on Truth* (1984), both accounts being based on letters which are in the *Complete Letters* but are not in the *Origins*. It demonstrates, to paraphrase Clark (1980), the almost unbelievable lengths to which Freud went to rationalize his faith in the scientific judgment of his indispensable authority-figure, Wilhelm Fliess. According to Anna Freud the relevant letters were omitted from the *Origins* 'since the story would have been incomplete and rather bewildering to the reader'. It has always been admitted that Freud was *kein Menschenkenner*, no judge of men, but it now appears that he could lose all common sense.

Another fateful consequence of Fliess's influence on Freud concerns Freud's *The Interpretation of Dreams*. It now appears that the original version of this book had as its core not the so-called Irma dream, which Schur and Masson have shown is really about Emma Eckstein's operation and Freud's need to exonerate Fliess, but another dream, which Freud removed in deference to Fliess's opinion that it was indiscreet. Details of this dream, which must have been about Freud's wife Martha, were apparently contained in one of the letters which Freud in 1937 said were missing from the set Marie Bonaparte had shown him. Nothing further is known about it, but the *Complete Letters* reveal that Freud valued it highly but accepted its removal meekly.

So the dream is condemned. Now that the sentence has been passed, however, I would like to shed a tear over it and confess that I regret it and that I have no hope of finding a better one as a substitute. As you know, a beautiful dream and no indiscretion – do not coincide.

He also wrote: 'The loss of the big dream that you eliminated is to be compensated for by the insertion of a small collection of dreams (harmless, absurd dreams; calculations and speeches in dreams; affects in dreams).' It is disconcerting to discover that one of the seminal works of the twentieth century lacks its centrepiece – and tantalizing too, since, in Masson's view 'There is still a faint hope that the letter will one day be found. It would no doubt be the most important letter of the collection, since it contains the only dream Freud ever analyzed completely.'

The *Complete Letters* also tell the story of how Freud came to believe that all his hysterical patients had been sexually abused in childhood by their fathers – and that his own four sisters and one brother had been abused by their father – and how he eventually abandoned this idea and replaced it by that of the Oedipus complex. However, as Masson has discussed this stage in Freud's thought in his recent *The Assault on Truth*, where he argues, to my mind unconvincingly, that Freud never really did abandon this seduction theory of the neuroses, and betrayed psychoanalysis by pretending to have done so, there is no need to pursue the matter further here.

As I have already mentioned, Masson's edition of the *Complete Letters of Sigmund Freud to Wilhelm Fliess: 1887–1904* is not a book that can be read on its own. Much of it is incomprehensible without reference to the introductions and footnotes in the *Origins* and Vol. I of the *Standard Edition*, and some of it remains incomprehensible even if one has these to hand: frequent allusions to Fliess's missing letters and unexplained nineteenth-century medical jargon render whole paragraphs totally opaque. It will, however, become an essential reference book for those who believe that there are still mysteries about Freud, and what made him tick, waiting to be discovered.

1985

R. W. Clark, *Freud: The Man and the Cause* (London: Jonathan Cape and Weidenfeld & Nicolson, 1980).

Henri F. Ellenberger, *The Discovery of the Unconscious* (New York: Basic Books, 1970).

Sigmund Freud, *The Origins of Psycho-Analysis*, ed. Marie Bonaparte, Anna Freud and Ernst Kris (London: Imago, 1954).
Extracts from the Fliess Papers in vol. I, *Standard Edition of the Complete Psychological Works* (London: The Hogarth Press, 1966).

Ernest Jones, *Sigmund Freud: Life and Work*, vol. I (London: The Hogarth Press, 1953).

J. M. Masson, *The Assault on Truth* (New York: Farrar, Straus & Giroux, 1984).

M. Schur, 'Some Additional "Day Residues" of the "Specimen Dream of Psychoanalysis"', in *Psychoanalysis – A General Psychology*, ed. R. M. Lowenstein *et al.* (New York: International Universities Press, 1966).

8

Masson's Assault on Freud

Early in 1984 Jeffrey Moussaieff Masson published *The Assault on Truth: Freud's Suppression of the Seduction Theory*,* in which he accused Freud of having been dishonest in abandoning his early theory that all hysterics have been sexually abused in childhood; and, furthermore, accused contemporary psychoanalysts, with their preoccupation with their patients' fantasies, of ignoring the frequency with which children, particularly female children, have suffered real, and not merely imagined, sexual abuse and violence in their childhoods. Later, in 1989, Masson went on to publish *Against Therapy*, in which he attacked, indiscriminately, all forms of psychotherapy.

Jeffrey Moussaieff Masson is, or perhaps rather was, a psychoanalyst – at present he is not, one gathers, a member of any psychoanalytical organization, does not see patients, and does not teach psychoanalysis anywhere. His book is a contribution to the early history of psychoanalysis, or rather would have been if he had not elected to present it in the form of a polemical attack on Freud, and on Freud's literary executors, notably Anna Freud, Ernest Jones and K. R. Eissler. Its title is, indeed, in a most peculiar way a misnomer, since Masson attacks Freud not for assaulting Truth but for retreating from it, and the assault described is Masson's on Freud, whom he accuses of cowardice, on his literary executors, whom he accuses of

---

* Jeffrey Moussaieff Masson, *The Assault on Truth: Freud's Suppression of the Seduction Theory* (New York: Farrar, Straus & Giroux, 1984).

suppressio veri, and on contemporary analysts, whom he accuses of ignoring the real violence inflicted on children.

It should perhaps be explained that Dr Masson was for a short while Projects Director of the Sigmund Freud Archives and as such had access to letters and documents which are still inaccessible to the general public; he was dismissed from this post after delivering a lecture in which he argued that Freud's abandonment of the theory that all his patients had been seduced as children had led to the 'present-day sterility of psychoanalysis throughout the world'. An account (hotly disputed by Masson, and later the subject of a libel case) of Masson's career, his alleged relations with Anna Freud and Kurt Eissler, Director of the Sigmund Freud Archives, and his reaction to his dismissal, was given in Janet Malcolm's *In The Freud Archives* (1984).

For those unfamiliar with the early history of psychoanalysis it must be explained that it began with the investigation of hysteria, a disorder common in the nineteenth century but now apparently rare. Freud originally maintained that the paralyses, faints, dizzy spells, deliria, etc., suffered by hysterics were not, as previous neurologists had insisted, due to exhaustion or degeneration of the nervous system, but were reactions to traumatic experiences, to disturbing events which the patient-victim had been unable to respond to and assimilate at the time. And he claimed, furthermore, that it was possible to cure hysteria by discovering what these traumatic experiences had been and helping the patient to remember them and to discharge the emotions appropriate to them.

Now, this idea that hysterical and, by extension, other neurotic symptoms were reactions to traumata obviously raised the question of what kind of experiences could be traumatizing, and by 1896 Freud had come to the conclusion that they were invariably sexual. In the April of that year he presented to the Society for Psychiatry and Neurology, in Vienna, a paper, 'The Aetiology of Hysteria', in which he asserted that 'without exception . . . at the bottom of every case of hysteria there are one or more occurrences of premature sexual experience, occurrences which belong to the earliest years of childhood but which can be reproduced through the work of psychoanalysis in spite of the intervening decades'. He went on to say that these premature sexual experiences had all occurred before the age of eight and that the eighteen cases (twelve female, six male) on which he based his paper could be divided into three groups, 'according to the origin of the sexual stimulation': those who had been assaulted by a stranger, those who had been seduced by 'some adult looking after the child – a nursery maid or governess, or tutor, or, unhappily all too often, a close relative', and those who had had a sexual relationship with another child, usually a brother, sister or cousin. Throughout this paper Freud assumes without question that he and his audience are agreed as to what they mean by the diagnostic label hysteria – which is an assumption that no contemporary lecturer on hysteria could make – and he explicitly states that all his eighteen cases had severe illnesses 'which threatened to make life impossible'. The implication is that they were much more disturbed than the kind of patient who consults a psychoanalyst today.

This paper, which is reprinted in full by Masson, apparently met with an icy reception, and Richard von Krafft-Ebing, who was in the chair, remarked that it sounded like a scientific fairy tale. And Freud himself soon began privately to have second thoughts on the matter. In a letter written on 21 September 1897 to his friend Wilhelm Fliess, the otorhino-laryngologist (ENT surgeon), Freud informed him that he no longer believed that all his hysterical patients had been seduced in childhood, one of the reasons for his disbelief being the fact that, if he continued to believe what his patients were telling him 'in all cases, the *father*, not excluding my own, had to be accused of being perverse'; a statement which suggests, first, that Freud had been less than outspoken when he read his paper, which refers not to fathers but to strangers, governesses, tutors and 'unhappily all too often, a close relative', and, secondly, that he must have arrived at the seduction theory of hysteria as much by self-analysis as by listening to his patients.

Masson, incidentally or perhaps not incidentally, does not mention the fact that Freud's father died in October 1896, that is, *after* Freud presented the seduction theory paper and before he wrote the disclaiming letter to Fliess. Freud, as is well known, believed that his father's death had been a turning point in his life: 'the most important event, the most poignant loss'. Masson also does not take full account of Jones's paraphrase of Freud's letter to Fliess, which reads: 'It was the awful truth that most – not all – of the seductions in childhood which his patients had revealed, and about which he had built his whole theory of hysteria, had never occurred,' a statement which implies that Freud continued to believe that some of his hysterical patients *had* been seduced in childhood.

For Jones, and indeed for most people, Freud's abandonment of the seduction theory was a victory for common sense and the beginning of a new era, one in which it became possible to elucidate the way in which fantasies can distort memory and in which infantile sexual wishes and parental attitudes combine to generate what we now call the Oedipus complex. As Anna Freud put it in a letter to Masson, 'keeping up the seduction theory would mean to abandon the Oedipus Complex, and with it the whole importance of phantasy life, conscious or unconscious phantasy. In fact, I think there would have been no psychoanalysis afterwards.'

But for Masson Freud's abandonment of the seduction theory was a disaster, a betrayal and a failure of courage. 'By shifting the emphasis from a real world of sadness, misery and cruelty to an internal stage on which actors performed invented dreams for an invisible audience of their own creation, Freud began a trend away from the real world that, it seems to me, has come to a dead halt in the present-day sterility of psychoanalysis throughout the world,' to quote from the lecture which precipitated his dismissal from his post with the Sigmund Freud Archives.

Despite Freud's letter to Fliess, which Freud can have had no reason to suppose would ever be published, and which in fact was not published until the 1950s, Masson seems to believe that Freud did not really and truly abandon the theory as erroneous, but put it out of his mind because he could not bear the professional isolation into which it was putting him. Hence Masson's subtitle 'The Suppression of the Seduction Theory', which implies both that Freud suppressed his own insight into the importance and frequency of child abuse and seduction and that the editors of Freud's letters to Fliess — Anna Freud, Marie Bonaparte and Ernst Kris — suppressed all references suggesting that Freud had continued to believe in the seduction theory after the date at which he was supposed to have abandoned it.

However, the evidence adduced by Masson is not very convincing. In fact he seems to have unearthed only one document which could be construed to mean that after the September 1897 letter abandoning the idea, Freud continued to believe that all his hysterical patients had been seduced by their fathers. But one obscure, rather gnomic letter does not make or break a theory; at the most it indicates that Freud was capable of wavering temporarily between two incompatible ideas. And this one letter was written only ten weeks after the one in which he had announced his disillusionment with the seduction theory.

However, in his search for evidence that Freud continued to believe in the seduction theory and that it deserves to be treated more seriously than it has been by most of Freud's followers, Masson, who combines the nose of a trufflehound with an incapacity to distinguish between facts, inferences and speculations, has unearthed some curious information which will, I think, permanently dent Freud's image.

First, he has unearthed data which suggest that Freud was more familiar with the forensic literature on child abuse, both sexual and what we now call child-battering, than anyone reading his *Collected Works* would suppose, and that he had almost certainly, when in Paris, attended autopsies on children who had died of non-accidental injuries. So he must have appreciated that assaults on children really do happen, known what their physical consequences could be, and his eventual incredulity about the stories his hysterical patients had told him cannot have derived from the sentimental idea that such things just don't happen.

Surprisingly, Masson makes no reference whatsoever to the modern forensic literature on child abuse, child-battering, paedophilia and incest, which he could have used to support the idea that contemporary analysts should consider the possibility that their patients' fantasies may be grounded in truth more often than, in his opinion, they do. Although Masson says that he is 'inclined to accept' the view that the incidence of sexual violence in the early lives of children may be as high as one in three in the general population and is 'undoubtedly higher among women who seek psychotherapy', he gives no evidence or references to support his inclination. His slide from being 'inclined to accept' to 'undoubtedly' is typical of his way of thinking.

Secondly, Masson adds a few details to the unedifying story of how Freud and Fliess bungled the treatment of Emma Eckstein, a young lady who must have been one of the eighteen patients on whom Freud based his paper 'The Aetiology of Hysteria'. In 1895 Fliess, with Freud's blessing, operated on Emma Eckstein's nose, hoping thereby to relieve her of various unspecified neurotic and gynaecological symptoms. After the operation she had severe nasal bleeding, which persisted until another surgeon removed 'at least half a meter of gauze' which Fliess had inadvertently left in her nose. Instead of being indignant at Fliess's incompetence, Freud persuaded himself that Emma Eckstein's post-operative bleeding had been hysterical in origin, and, according to Masson, Freud's need to persuade himself that Fliess's surgical assault on Emma Eckstein had not really happened, and that her post-operative bleeding was the product of her neurotic imagination, contributed to his later belief that all tales of assault recounted by hysterical patients were fantasies.

Most of this story has already been told by Max Schur, and, as far as facts go, Masson's only additions are that Emma Eckstein remained permanently disfigured, that two to three years after the operation she was herself analysing a patient under Freud's supervision, and that she preserved and left to her nephew (who gave them to the Library of Congress) fourteen letters from Freud, dating from 1895 to 1910 and including a prescription for 'boric acid for the vagina'. He also argues that Freud was preoccupied with her to the end of his days, as indeed he may well have been.

However, Masson's technique of confusing facts with speculation does not inspire confidence. After mentioning that Emma Eckstein wrote a book entitled *The Question of Sexuality in Child Rearing*, in which she used an invented letter from a mother to a son to express some of her ideas, Masson goes on:

It is not beyond the realm of possibility that Emma Eckstein had an illegitimate child and that her letter is in fact based on reality. If the child was ten at the time this book was written, then she would have given birth in 1894, during her analysis. Being in analysis, she would have told Freud, and possibly nobody else. I must stress that none of the six people I spoke to who knew Emma Eckstein had ever heard any such rumour. Nor do I believe this is anything more than speculation. But it is one more piece of evidence that the mystery surrounding Emma Eckstein has by no means been resolved.

But a speculation cannot be a piece of evidence, and the passage has too many 'if's' and 'woulds' and 'possibles' in it to be taken seriously. It also contains an insinuation: an illegitimate child must have a father as well as a mother. Although Masson's avowed aim in discussing the case of Emma Eckstein is to demonstrate that Freud had a powerful subjective motive for wishing to deny the real effects of assaults, it is hard to resist the temptation that Masson is also engaged in stirring up dirt in the hope that some will stick.

Thirdly, Masson marshals evidence to suggest that Freud's repudiation of his disciple Ferenczi and of his 1932 paper 'Confusion of Tongues between Adults and the Child' was due to Ferenczi having rediscovered the truth of the seduction theory that he had suppressed thirty-five years previously. According to Ferenczi, 'Even children of respected, high-minded puritanical families fall victim to real rape much more frequently than one had dared to suspect. Either the parents themselves seek substitution for their lack of (sexual) satisfaction in this pathological manner, or else trusted persons such as relatives (uncles, aunts, grandparents), tutors, servants, abuse the ignorance and innocence of children.' This corresponds exactly to what Freud had said in his 1896 paper, but Ferenczi goes on to add something that Freud did not say: 'The obvious objection that we are dealing with sexual fantasies of the child himself, that is, with hysterical lies, unfortunately is weakened by the multitude of confessions of this kind, on the part of patients in analysis, to assaults on children.' But, curiously, Ferenczi does not go on to cite any of the 'multitude of confessions' made to him by patients in analysis but to the much weaker 'Thus I was not surprised when a short time ago an educator known for his high-minded philanthropy came to see me in a state of veritable despair to tell me that thus far he had been unfortunate enough to discover five families of good society in which the governesses lived in a regular conjugal state with nine-to-eleven year old boys.'

Characteristically, Masson does not perceive that this passage from Ferenczi does not survive critical scrutiny and could, indeed, be used as a textbook example of sloppy, crooked thinking. First, Ferenczi has 'children of respected, high-minded puritanical families' being raped 'much more frequently than one had dared to suspect' – how frequently would that be? – and later in life telling their analyst about it. Then, to rebut the argument that these patients might have been telling 'hysterical lies', he refers to 'the multitudes of confessions . . . to assaults on children' made to him by adult patients in analysis, thereby leaving open such questions as 'Did a multitude of patients make single confessions?', 'Did each of a few patients make a multitude of confessions?', and 'Did patients who had themselves been raped as children make a contribution to the multitude of confessions?' And then in support of the truth of the multitude of confessions made to him, Ferenczi cites the hearsay evidence of 'an educator known for his high-minded philanthropy' that five nine- to eleven-year-old boys of good society were living 'in a regular conjugal state' with their governesses. Now, it may or may not be a good thing for nine- to eleven-year-old boys to sleep with their governesses, but 'living in a regular conjugal state' with a governess is certainly neither rape nor assault, though it does suggest that some seduction may have been going on.

I have dwelt on this passage and dissected it in some detail because it is a good example not only of how Ferenczi thought but also of how Masson does think – the translation from the original German is, incidentally, by Masson himself – the thesis that neuroses are the result of childhood sexual traumatic experiences being sustained in each case by the tendentious use of language, by the refusal to distinguish between such concepts as rape, assault and seduction, and even by failure to distinguish between 'some', 'many' and 'all'; the fact that some children are indeed raped, assaulted and seduced is inflated into a theory that all neurosis is caused by assaults.

Masson's account of Freud's repudiation of Ferenczi is also marred by dirt-stirring. Freud is presented not only as a hypocrite and a prig but also as thinking that all patients are riff-raff (*Gesindel*) – the evidence is one remark of Freud's recorded in Ferenczi's diary – while Ferenczi is inadvertently (I think) made to sound pathetic and silly. Even before he became an analyst he had a tendency to 'sexual playing about with patients', he saw one of his analytical patients, a beautiful American dancer, for four or five sessions a day, sat another on his lap, gave yet another a doll to comfort her, fell in love with a patient but married her mother, and went through life longing for the parental love he had never received as a child – he was 'a middle child among eleven or thirteen others'. As in his account of Freud's relationship with Emma Eckstein, Masson cites details from unpublished letters and diaries without giving enough of their personal and social context for the reader to be able to know how to evaluate them.

Masson's reasons for wishing to resurrect the seduction theory do not emerge in this book. As he is a Sanskrit scholar not a doctor of medicine, and can have treated only a few patients himself, it cannot be that clinical or professional experience has driven him to return to Freud's original hypothesis. He tells us that even as a student it had never seemed right to him that Freud would not believe his patients and 'I did not agree that the seduction scenes represented as memories were only fantasies, or memories of fantasies.' He seems, indeed, to operate with a naive, literal-minded antithesis between memories which are real and fantasies which are imaginary. In his view, if a patient recounts a 'memory' of a sexual assault or seduction, the analyst is lacking in respect for the patient and accusing him of lying if he questions its literal truth; it does not seem to occur to him that there can be a dialectical relationship between experience and fantasy, each affecting the other, or that apparent memories may express metaphorical truths and fantasies contain both literal and metaphorical truths. As a result he has to believe that all patients have been literally assaulted or seduced, and he lacks the conceptual framework with which to explore the ways in which psychological and emotional violations and manipulations may be expressed in sexual imagery. Many patients must have been buggered up by their parents, but only a few, I think, have been literally buggered by them.

Rather surprisingly, Masson does not refer to the fact that many child-rearing and surgical procedures involve literal violations of bodily integrity and must inevitably be experienced by small children as assaults, quite regardless of the conscious or unconscious motives of the parents and surgeons who inflict such traumata on their children. This is a curious omission, since it would be possible to resurrect the traumatic theory of neurosis on the basis of the mishandling of small children. In England, D. W. Winnicott went a long way in this direction.

Lastly, it must be said, I think, that there is a persecutory slant in Masson's thinking. The idea that neuroses are due to violations inflicted on children by sexually perverse and dissatisfied adults attributes blame to the offending adults, who are cast in the role of villains. But in fact, of course, many patients are the victims not of malice or cruelty or perversion but of tragedy. Parents may die, or themselves be grieving the deaths of their own parents, or may have to leave home for reasons of work or war, thereby producing anxious, insecure, depressive patients, whose illnesses are nobody's fault. If Masson had really wanted to reintroduce a traumatic theory of neurosis, he would have done better to base it on Bowlby's work on separation and loss, instead of attempting to resuscitate Freud's seduction theory. As it is, he has produced a book that is distasteful, misguided and at times silly.

1984

John Bowlby, *Attachment and Loss*, vol. III (London: The Hogarth Press, 1980). *Loss, Sadness and Depression* (London: The Hogarth Press, 1980). Sandor Ferenczi, 'Confusion of Tongues between Adults and the Child', English translation in *International Journal of Psychoanalysis*, vol. 30 (1949).

Sigmund Freud, Letter to Wilhelm Fliess in *The Complete Letters of Sigmund Freud to Wilhelm Fliess 1887–1904*, ed. Jeffrey Moussaief Masson (Cambridge, Mass.: Harvard University Press, 1985).

The Origins of Psychoanalysis, ed. Marie Bonaparte, Anna Freud and Ernst Kris (London: Imago, 1954).

Ernest Jones, *Sigmund Freud: Life and Work* (London: The Hogarth Press, 1953).

Janet Malcolm, *In the Freud Archives* (London: Jonathan Cape, 1984).

Max Schur, 'Some Additional "Day Residues" of the "Specimen Dream of Psychoanalysis"', in *Psychoanalysis – A General Psychology*, ed. R. M. Lowenstein *et al.* (New York: International Universities Press, 1966).

D. W. Winnicott, *Collected Papers* (London: Tavistock, 1958).

9

Freud for Historians

Since *Freud for Historians** appeared in 1985, Peter Gay has published *Freud: A Life for Our Time* (1988), which was intended as the updated successor to Ernest Jones's three-volume *Sigmund Freud: Life and Work* (1953–7) and has been accepted as such by the psychoanalytical establishment. As Paul Roazen, in *Encountering Freud* (1990), has said of him, 'He sees himself as trying to lead the loyalist cause within the history of psychoanalysis . . . [he] appears to be an apologist putting what he conceives as the best face on everything connected to Freud.' Gay's *Reading Freud* (1990), a collection of essays most of which started life as lectures to audiences of psychoanalysts, assumes that their writer and readers share a common veneration for Freud and a preparedness to accept his weaknesses and failings as easily forgivable foibes. Having said so much about Gay, I must add that two earlier books by him, *Weimar Culture: The Outsider as Insider* (1968) and *Freud, Jews and other Germans* (1978), both struck me as most impressive.

In his largely autobiographical Preface Peter Gay tells us he first became interested in psychoanalysis 'as a system of ideas and an auxiliary discipline' some thirty years ago, and that he entered the Western New England Institute for Psychoanalysis as a research candidate in 1976, undergoing a didactic analysis lasting several years. Professor Gay is, therefore, not an analyst turned historian, nor indeed an historian turned analyst, but a lifelong historian convinced that certain psychoanalytical ideas

* Peter Gay, *Freud for Historians* (Oxford: Oxford University Press, 1985).

can and should be used by historians to illuminate the past. As a result, as he himself says, he occupies a vulnerable, threatened position; the history establishment is on the whole hostile towards psychohistory, while 'most psychoanalysts can scarcely repress their suspicions of what they think of, a little grudgingly, as "applied analysis". The psychoanalytic historian must be prepared to face skepticism from Freud's followers almost as much as from his denigrators.'

It appears to me that the problems faced by Professor Gay and other psychohistorians arise from two facts: first, that there are so many pasts and therefore so many branches and kinds of history, and, secondly, that human nature is so various and variegated that psychoanalysis, to the extent that it has achieved a conceptual framework that reflects this variety, has generated so many ideas. As a result, anyone venturing into the troubled waters of psychohistory has to discover and select which psychoanalytical ideas are relevant and appropriate to the period or branch of history he wishes to study. (Presumably an analyst turned historian might proceed the opposite way round and select a period of history which seemed to him to exemplify with peculiar clarity some psychoanalytical idea he wished to popularize and illustrate. This is indeed what Erik Erikson did in *Young Man Luther*.)

Now Professor Gay is at present engaged on 'a study of nineteenth-century bourgeois culture from a psychoanalytical perspective' (*The Bourgeois Experience: Victoria to Freud*, 6 volumes, of which two, *Education of the Senses* (1984) and *The Tender Passion* (1986), have already appeared), and I see no reason to doubt that the particular set of psychoanalytical ideas that he recommends to the attention of historians in *Freud for Historians* is in fact the appropriate one for his particular enterprise; but he is, I think, wrong in implying, as he does, that it is the set required by all historians or even that it constitutes the central core of psychoanalytical thinking.

The psychoanalytical concepts that Gay wishes to propagate among historians are roughly those which Freud developed in his later writings from 1920 onwards and from which contemporary psychoanalytical ego-psychology derives: the idea that the mind is a tripartite structure, consisting of the id (which contains two groups of instinctual drives, the sexual and the aggressive), the ego (which is adapted towards the outside world), and the super-ego (which contains precipitates of parental and other authority figures); the idea that groups are held together by the identifications of their members with one another and with an idealized paternal leader; and the idea that the ego uses a variety of defence mechanisms to protect itself from being overwhelmed by sexual and aggressive drives and that civilization is based on repression and sublimation of these instinctual drives.

Although these Freudian concepts are clearly and often elegantly described, I doubt whether Gay's presentation of them will fire the imagination of historians in the way that he hopes it will. This is largely because he fails to give adequate accounts of a number of earlier and more basic Freudian concepts without which Freud's ego-psychology appears static and unimaginative; Gay has little to say about fantasy, symbolism, sublimation, guilt and anxiety, and I doubt whether any reader of *Freud for Historians* not already familiar with psychoanalysis would grasp that, in Freud's view, the id and the ego function in entirely different and incompatible ways, the former using images and symbols ordered according to what he called the primary processes (condensation and displacement) which ignore the categories of space and time, the latter using words ordered discursively according to the rules of logic and syntax. Nor would he discover that many contemporary analysts think that Freud assumed too sharp an antithesis between the ego and the id and their respective modes of functioning.

In concentrating so exclusively on one particular phase in Freud's thinking – and indeed in entitling his book *Freud for Historians* not *Psychoanalysis for Historians* – Professor Gay has, I think, failed to use his historian's imagination. If he had approached psychoanalysis not as a single set of ideas produced by one man but as an intellectual movement which began in a specific milieu at the end of the nineteenth century and has expanded and developed in various directions in various countries – and has displayed, like so many other movements, internal contradictions and divisive tensions – he might have discovered that psychoanalysis has explored more areas of human experience than are accounted for by Freud's ego-psychology and has produced other clusters of ideas which could well be of as much use to historians as the one to which he has restricted himself, if not more.

Two in particular strike me as being likely to be of interest to historians. First, there is the literature which elucidates the origins and the interrelationships of the various emotions of self-regard and the sense of identity – raised and lowered self-esteem, pride, shame and humiliation – emotions which Freud, with his preoccupation with guilt, did not consider in detail. Fortunately for historians, the best and most illuminating book on this area, Helen Merrell Lynd's *On Shame and the Search for Identity* (1958), is the work of an author who, though well informed about psychoanalysis, was nonetheless deeply grounded in literature and history. The psychodynamics of pride and shame should, it seems to me, be of particular interest to historians studying nationalism, militarism, chivalry and gentility.

Secondly, there is the psychoanalytical tradition of concern with depression, despair, grief, mania, elation and ecstasy. This tradition started with the work of Karl Abraham in the early 1920s and is at present represented by the object-relations school, which flourishes in Great Britain and is beginning to attract attention in the United States. Professor Gay has certainly heard of this school, since he mentions representatives of it several times, mostly in footnotes, but he has not, I think, appreciated the extent to which it diverges from the phase of Freud's thinking to which he is attached, and it seems not to have occurred to him that the psychology of depression and mania – and such concepts as the depressive position and manic defence – could be of use to historians in general and of particular interest to historians of totalitarian, religious and chiliastic movements.

1986

10

The Wound and the Bow

When this review of Leonard Shengold's *Soul Murder: The Effects of Childhood Abuse and Deprivation*** appeared in the *New York Review of Books*, it was under the title 'The Wound and the Bow', an allusion to Edmund Wilson's 1941 book of that name. Wilson had used the Greek myth of Philoctetes to describe the relationship between artistic creativity and trauma: Philoctetes was the best archer in the Greek armies besieging Troy, but he suffered from a chronic, suppurating, foul-smelling wound which his companions in arms found intolerable. He was, therefore, abandoned in the island of Lemnos, where his wound eventually healed. But when he returned to the Greek army he was no longer the superlative archer he had formerly been. Readers will discover that this myth has indeed some relevance to parts of Shengold's book. (The present text is a conflation of the text as I originally wrote it and the text as sub-edited for publication.)

In his Introduction Dr Shengold confesses that he is 'fond of meandering designs; this book proceeds more by association than by orderly progression'. In his Acknowledgements he states that in *Soul Murder* and in *Halo in the Sky* (1988) he has 'published most of the ideas and discoveries that have been derived from my practice of psychoanalysis over the past thirty years', and elsewhere he states that unspecified sections have already appeared as articles in four different psychoanalytical journals.

* Leonard Shengold, *Soul Murder: The Effects of Childhood Abuse and Deprivation* (New Haven and London: Yale University Press, 1989).

Dr Shengold is, then, a distinguished psychoanalyst (he is Clinical Professor of Psychiatry at the New York University School of Medicine) who, after being in practice for over thirty years, has now collected a sample of the various papers he has written and woven them into the semblance of a book (as opposed to a volume of Collected Papers). However, despite the patchwork, the repetitiousness and the 'meandering design', this book does have a recurrent unifying theme, vividly described by its title *Soul Murder*.

Soul murder is my dramatic designation for a certain category of traumatic experience: instances of repetitive and chronic over-stimulation, alternating with emotional deprivation, that are deliberately brought about by another individual. The term does not define a clinical entity; it applies more to pathogenic circumstances than to specific effects.

Although the concept of soul murder is a vivid *metaphor* for describing the actions of persons who deliberately abuse, batter, deprive, torment, torture and brainwash helpless victims, it is nonetheless misleading in certain respects. Actual murder leaves the victim dead, with no possibility of living or reviving to tell the tale, while the victims of what Shengold, following highly respectable literary and psychoanalytical precedents, calls soul murder are still alive and may under certain circumstances or psychological constellations be able to tell the tale, and thereby regain the spirit which their 'murderers' sought to crush and recover the sense of identity and personal autonomy of which their 'murderers' sought to deprive them.

Shengold discusses Kipling, Chekhov, Dostoevsky, and Orwell as victims of soul murder, and creates confusion for himself (and even more for his readers) by trying to explain how victims of soul murder can become creative artists. Part of the confusion arises, it seems to me, because he oscillates between the idea that an individual either has or has not been soul-murdered, in which case he either is or is not psychically dead – which is what the murder metaphor implies – and recognition that psychical damage, traumatic experiences, vary in their intensity from slight to extreme. In fact, of course, Shengold, despite his metaphor of murder, realizes quite clearly that the kinds of experience he is describing are all quantifiable in both intensity and duration. The real point about situations that perhaps merit the name 'soul murder' is that the behaviour of the 'murderer' is beyond the empathic range of the average normal neurotic – Shengold insists more than once that everyone who is not psychotic is neurotic – and the reaction of the victim involves the use of an impreessive array of defences:

an extraordinary power of disassociation from feeling and experience; autohypnotic states; compromised identity, with vertical ego splitting allowing for phenomena analogous to the doublethink and crimestop of Orwell's *1984*; a paranoid potentiality (if you can't trust your parents, whom can you trust); superego defenses with simultaneous overpermissiveness and a strong need for punishment . . .

The pain he or she has suffered *seems* to have been obliterated at the cost of loss of freedom of emotional expression.

The idea that 'soul murder' is a quantifiable experience is expressed clearly at the beginning of the chapter on Kipling, where Shengold writes: 'Soul Murder can be overwhelmingly or minimally effected; it can be partial, diluted, chronic or subtle. Kipling's case involves his desertion by good parents and their replacement by bad, persecutory guardians.' Surely the first sentence in this quotation should read: 'Soul murder can be either overwhelming or slight; it can be partial or complete, diluted or concentrated, chronic or acute, subtle or crude'?

Clarity of thought is not one of Shengold's gifts, and despite reading this chapter more than once it still remains unclear to me whether he really believes that Kipling's parents were as 'good' as Kipling himself thought they were or the guardians as 'bad' as Kipling described them in his fiction, or whether he thinks that Kipling was a great writer despite, or as a result of, his childhood experiences of abuse and deprivation.

The chapter on Kipling does, however, give Shengold the opportunity for quotations which describe with poetic clarity and intensity the predicament, the emotional scarring, of the kind of patient who has been his abiding preoccupation. For instance:

When young lips have drunk deep of the bitter waters of Hate, Suspicion, and Despair, all the Love in the world will not wholly take away that knowledge; though it may turn darkened eyes for a while to the light, and teach Faith where no Faith was.

(Curiously, this passage from 'Baa, Baa, Black Sheep' is both misquoted and misdated by Shengold, who gives 'your' for 'young' and the date of composition as 1988!) Another example is the poem 'The Mother's Son' (1928), which describes a patient in an asylum looking at his reflection in a mirror:

> And it was *not* disease or crime
> Which got him landed there
> But because They laid on My Mother's Son
> More than a man could bear.

Shengold's text reads 'than any man could bear', and one of the interpretations he offers of this poem, that the beardedness of the face in the mirror shocks the viewer because he had expected or hoped to see his childhood hairless face, is invalidated by one of the verses which he does *not* quote:

> They pushed him into a Mental Home
> And that is like the grave;
> For they do not let you sleep upstairs
> And you aren't allowed to shave.

Some of the complexities and tortuosities of Shengold's accounts of soul murder in the lives of writers arise from the fact that he both has and has not accepted Freud's reluctant admission that 'Before the problem of the creative artist analysis must, alas, lay down its arms.' On the one hand, he quotes it with approval, but incompletely and in a garbled context; on the other hand, a few pages later he can write: 'in some still unanalyzable way Chekhov can transcend and transform his neurosis – at least in his art. We are confronting a magnificent psychological gift and talent, not pathology; this is terra incognita for the psychoanalyst; another Freud is needed.' And of Dickens he writes: 'If one had the facts, however, one might find his talents and strengths as well as his subject matter, linked genetically to his early traumatic experiences.' When one remembers that this book is based on papers written for psychoanalytical journals and that some of them must also have been read to audiences of psychoanalysts, one is forced to believe that the spirit of Freud's original analytical imperialism is alive and well in American psychoanalytical circles.

Another reason for Shengold's obscurity is one which will, I suspect, baffle all readers who have not at some time immersed themselves in the history and politics of the psychoanalytical movement. In writing about child abuse and soul murder he has entered an area of theoretical controversy about the relative importance of fantasy and experience in the genesis of neurosis. In 1984, in *The Assault on Truth: Freud's Suppression of the Seduction Theory*, Jeffrey Masson argued that Freud had been right in asserting, as he had in *The Aetiology of Hysteria* (1896), that all neurotics have been abused sexually in their childhood, and had been dishonest in abandoning this idea in favour of the socially innocuous one that children regularly have Oedipal fantasies of sexual contact with their parents. By writing this book Masson was asserting, specifically, that, since neurosis is common, sexual abuse of children must also be common, and, generally, that neuroses are the result of real events in childhood and not of fantasies created in childhood, as most orthodox, mainstream analysts seemed to believe.

According to Janet Malcolm's *In the Freud Archives* (1984), Shengold was initially most impressed by Masson and had even got up at a meeting Masson had been addressing to say, apparently seriously, 'I've never heard of this man, but he's a find. Canada has sent us a national treasure,' but as he got to know him better, he became disenchanted. So, although Shengold clearly believes that child abuse and soul murder are not uncommon, he is at pains to make it clear that he does not agree with Masson's thesis that child abuse is ubiquitous or with his denial of the pathogenic power of fantasy.

Shengold also dissociates himself from Robert Fliess. (Uninformed readers are warned that two Fliesses, Wilhelm and Robert, father and son, Berlin nasal surgeon and New York psychoanalyst, friend and correspondent of Freud and elder colleague of Shengold, feature in this book, but are distinguished in neither the text nor the index. Shengold presumably assumed that his analyst readers would recognize immediately which Fliess he was referring to, while the indexer can have had no reason to suppose that there were two of them.) Shengold has evidently been much influenced theoretically by Robert Fliess, but Fliess (like Masson) also believed that all his patients had been seduced in childhood and that most of their parents had been ambulant psychotics. Shengold takes them both on:

> How frequent are the seduction and abuse of children? They are certainly more common than had been realized for decades. Now that people are increasingly aware of the fact of child abuse, accounts fill our newspapers, magazines, and even television (as well as the psychiatric literature). It makes no sense to me that all neurotics (and this means everyone) have been traumatically abused and seduced in their childhood, as Freud first assumed and as Fliess and Masson assert. Soul Murder has certainly not happened to everyone, but this book is evidence of my conviction that overt, substantial parental seduction and deprivation are frequent.

Although Shengold states clearly and courteously the extent of both his indebtedness to, and disagreement with, Jeffrey Masson and Robert Fliess, the same cannot be said of his attitude towards Morton Schatzman, the American psychotherapist working in London, England, who in 1973 published *Soul Murder: Persecution in the Family*. In this book Schatzman discussed the delusions of persecution by God described by Daniel Paul Schreber in his *Memoirs of My Nervous Illness* (1903), which Freud in a famous paper ('Psycho-analytic notes on an autobiographical account of a case of paranoia (dementia paranoides)', 1911) had interpreted as the result of Schreber's passive homosexual love for his father. Schatzman suggested that the delusions were better interpreted as replicas and transformations of physical assaults that his father had inflicted upon him in childhood; and that his father, Moritz Schreber, far from being an admirable person 'by no means unsuitable for transfiguration into a God in the affectionate memory of the son', as Freud had described him, had been a sadistic tyrant. The book engendered considerable controversy, with Schatzman, on the one hand, arguing that Schreber's delusions of persecution were the direct result of maltreatment and abuse by his sadistic father, and the orthodox analysts, on the other hand, defending Freud's original thesis that delusions of persecution are vicissitudes of passive homosexual drives. It would seem, however, that both parties to this controversy have been both ignorant and misguided. According to Han Israëls, the Dutch sociologist whose historical study of the Schreber family has recently been translated into English (*Schreber: Father and Son*, 1989), Moritz Schreber was not as famous as both Schatzman and Freud had assumed, was not such a paragon as Freud has believed nor as vicious as Schatzman painted him, and neither of their aetiological theories stands up to critical scrutiny.

However, despite the fact that it was Schatzman who first raised the issue of soul murder and started the controversy in which Shengold himself took part, Schatzman's *Soul Murder* is not mentioned anywhere in the text of Shengold's *Soul Murder* – though it is included in the Bibliography.

Shengold's reason for ignoring someone with whose work he must be familiar and the title of whose book he has borrowed must, I think, be that Schatzman is an outsider, who is not and never has been a psychoanalyst, and is, therefore, not a member of that elect group, the American (or should it be the New York?) psychoanalytical establishment, for whom Shengold writes and whose approval he needs.

Janet Malcolm has described Shengold as occupying a special corner in the analytic avant-garde. 'On the one hand, he shares the avant-garde's concern for "people who have been unloved, ill-used, and deprived" . . . but on the other he does not share its (variously expressed) need to meddle with orthodox theory and practice. Almost alone among analysts who have dedicated themselves to the repair of seriously damaged souls, Shengold has remained comfortable with regular Freudian psychoanalysis.'

Although he is undoubtedly concerned with the unloved, illused and deprived, the clinical material on which *Soul Murder* is based is not of the most extreme. He writes:

> My material will seem mild indeed to those dealing with battered and sexually assaulted children who turn up in police stations and hospital

emergency rooms. I will describe people who were assaulted as children and have been scarred, but who have enough ego strength to maintain their psychological development and have summoned the considerable mental strength needed to present themselves as patients for psychoanalysis . . . I have not studied any of the countless number who have ended as derelicts, in madhouses, or in jails, or those who have not even survived an abused childhood.

However, the material is dramatic enough. Of the seventeen patients, twelve males and five females, discussed in some detail, twelve had been abused in childhood by their mothers and three by their fathers, the other two being a woman who had been seduced at the age of five by a man who was not her father, and a man who had been grossly neglected by both parents but not abused. Although the sample is not large enough to be statistically significant, Shengold's findings do nonetheless suggest that the popular idea that child abuse is essentially a matter of fathers abusing their daughters is something of a myth. Both sons and daughters can, it seems, be sexually abused by their mothers, the kinds of maternal abuse mentioned including genital exhibitionism, fellatio, and anal rape masquerading as therapeutic administration of enemas.

The one incestuous relationship described by Shengold was between a mother and her pubertal son; it was initiated by the mother, enjoyed by the son, but terminated by the mother after a few weeks when he had his first ejaculation. One effect on the son of this brief encounter was 'guilt-ridden arrogance'. In later life his wife was often provoked into saying to him, 'You know, you are not of royal birth.' Not surprisingly, Shengold's discussion of this case includes allusions to *Oedipus Rex*.

In addition to describing the soul murders partially inflicted on four writers and seventeen patients, Shengold also discusses a variety of cognate topics: the rat, both as an actual animal which under stress kills and eats its own kind and as an apt and much-used symbol of projected oral aggression; teeth in folklore and as attributed to the 'bad breast'; the sphinx as a symbol of what I would call a combined parent figure but which Shengold calls 'the primal parent'; the myth of Oedipus; the Schreber case; Kaspar Hauser; auto-hypnosis; quasi-delusions occurring in the normal ('we neurotics all have them'); and many others. Unfortunately the combination of his wish to record everything he has discovered in thirty years of analytical practice and his affection for 'meandering designs' often makes him hard to follow; his erudition is impressive, but also overwhelming and distracting.

1990

Soul Murder and Survival – Bruno Bettelheim

In this essay on Bruno Bettelheim, which is based on reviews of two of his books,* I have discussed only his work with autistic children and, more briefly, his reactions to the year he spent in concentration camps. A complete picture of his life and work would have to include, *inter alia*, his writings on fairy tales (*The Uses of Enchantment*, 1977), his attack on the English trans-lators of Freud who, he claimed, obscured the essential human-ism of Freud's work, notably by translating the German word *Seele* as 'mind' not 'soul' (*Freud and Man's Soul*, 1982), and his writings on the holocaust (*Surviving and Other Essays*, 1979), and *Surviving the Holocaust*, 1986). There is something as yet undisclosed about Bettelheim's relationship with the psycho-analytical movement; one hopes that an informed biography will be available before too long.

The late Professor Bruno Bettelheim, who died by his own hand in 1989, was an authority on the capacity to survive extreme situations. His well-known early book *The Informed Heart: The Human Condition in Modern Mass Society* (1960) was largely based on his own personal experiences and observations while a prisoner in Dachau and Buchenwald and was in the main an analysis of what decided whether a person lived or died in a concentration camp. In it he was concerned not so much with the physical capacity to survive brutality and torture as with the

* Bruno Bettelheim, *The Empty Fortress: Infantile Autism and the Birth of the Self* (New York: Free Press, 1967; London, Collier-Macmillan, 1968), and *A Home for the Heart* (London, Thames & Hudson, 1974).

psychological factors which determine whether a person will be able to resist demoralization in a setting in which he has ceased to be in any way a free agent, which is designed to reduce him to a nonentity, and which has no wish that he should go on living.

The same preoccupation with the response of human beings to situations which sap the will to live also pervaded *The Empty Fortress: Infantile Autism and the Birth of the Self* (1967). This is an account of his therapeutic work with autistic children at the Chicago Orthogenic School, of which he was Director from 1944 to 1973. It was his conviction that autistic children have been brought up in families in which they have never been allowed to be themselves, and in which they sensed, perhaps from the very beginning of life, that their parents wished that they did not exist. The 'empty fortress' of the title is the psyche of such children, which he likened to a fortress designed to preserve the possibility of a self which might emerge later in an environment which would not be felt to threaten its existence. (This is similar to Winnicott's idea that 'false selves' function as 'caretaker selves' until such time as it is safe for the real self to emerge.) Before considering Bettelheim's reasons for taking this view of the nature and origin of an illness which many, perhaps most, psychiatrists believe to be organic, a brief account of childhood psychosis and infantile autism is perhaps necessary.

Although childhood psychosis is a rarity in comparison with childhood neurosis, the devastating effects it has on the child and on his family, and the possibility that it may provide fundamental evidence about emotional and intellectual development, combine to give it an importance out of all proportion to the number of children affected. Descriptive psychiatry recognizes four kinds of childhood psychosis: schizophrenia and manic-depressive psychosis, both of which resemble the adult diseases; the symbiotic psychosis first described by Margaret Mahler, in which the child remains in emotional contact with its mother but with her only; and infantile autism, in which the child makes contact with no one. Bettelheim himself would also have included among the childhood psychoses infantile marasmus, the wasting away unto death which afflicts emotionally deprived children in institutions. These he likens to the 'moslems' of the concentration camps, who resigned themselves fatalistically to the inevitability of death and faded away.

Autistic children are often suspected at first of being deaf or mentally defective, but they neither look stupid nor does their ability to handle things support the idea of an innate intellectual defect. Their most striking features are their 'extreme autistic loneliness', their self-sufficiency and their obsessive need to control the inanimate objects in their environment. They also display disturbances of speech; some are mutes, while others construct their sentences curiously and are incapable of using the words 'I' or 'yes'.

According to Leo Kanner, who first described the condition in 1943, they come of notably intelligent stock and tend to have parents who are intellectual but inhuman. These parents are, Kanner said, 'more at home in the world of abstractions than in the world of people . . . They treat their children about as meticulously as they treat their automobiles . . . it is possible to speak of them as successfully autistic adults.'

Kanner thought that autism was an inherited disorder occurring in families in which a high IQ was also inherited, but Bettelheim disagreed on both points. He thought that the incidence of autism is higher than is usually supposed, but that it is only those autistic children who have intelligent and well-informed parents capable of seeking out specialized clinics who get correctly diagnosed; while those whose parents are unintelligent and ill-educated acquire other diagnoses, usually schizophrenia or mental deficiency. He also maintained – and this was his essential thesis – that autism is a psychogenic illness capable of a psychoanalytical explanation, the symptoms of which should be regarded as defences against threats to autistic children's identity and as responses to the failure of their parents to welcome them into the world.

Bettelheim's sense of conviction about this derived from the intensity and intimacy of his contacts with autistic children. Prior to the year he spent in concentration camps he had one and sometimes two autistic children living in his home in Vienna, and prior to writing *The Empty Fortress* he had had over twenty years of contact with them as Director of the Chicago Orthogenic School.

Although the Chicago Orthogenic School was run along psychoanalytic lines, the children there did not have analytical treatment in any formal sense, the whole setting rather than particular sessions being utilized for therapy. The children were given every opportunity to discover themselves as free agents and to learn that the basic self-enhancing physical activities of childhood – eating, defecating, urinating, walking, talking – are acts that can be performed because they themselves will it and wish it, not because they are behaviour-patterns on which adults insist. In such a setting children can, Bettelheim believed, acquire the trust in other human beings which more fortunate children learn by discovering that their mothers respond spontaneously to their needs, and the sense of autonomy which derives from learning how to master one's own body for one's own sake.

In his theoretical justification of the School's therapeutic methods Bettelheim followed Erik Erikson in maintaining that the first two stages in the birth of the self are those of basic trust and autonomy, which correspond to the oral and anal phases of classical psychoanalytical theory. During both these phases autistics had, in Bettelheim's view, been physically cared for by parents who had failed, for a variety of reasons, to respond to them imaginatively and humanly. It was not exposure to cruelty, hatred, or material deprivation, but the negative trauma of not being recognized and reacted to which was responsible for their conviction 'that there is nothing at all one can do about a world that offers some satisfaction, though not those one desires'.

The evidence on which Bettelheim based this conception of infantile autism is contained in the case histories which form the bulk of The Empty Fortress. Although readers of this book who lack relevant clinical experience or, even more, who are not at home with psychoanalytical jargon will miss a lot, none can fail to be overwhelmed by admiration for the heroism and persistence shown by Bettelheim and his numerous co-workers. Not only do these children make enormous demands on the imagination and patience of their therapists, they also hit, bite, defecate, and urinate on them (one staff member required medical treatment for human bites twelve times in a single year) and may continue to do so for years before a trusting, responsive human being begins to emerge.

Although many, perhaps most, psychotherapists find work of this intensity heart-breaking, despair was not an emotion to which Bettelheim was prone; indeed, some of his asides reveal a certain contempt for people who despair and then claim it as evidence of their own superior sensibility. He was also fortified by an enormous faith in his own insight, and like many other psychotherapists who allow themselves to empathize with psychotic and primitive experience, he sometimes wrote as though he had a private line to God. This led him at times into asserting that he had a deeper appreciation of the active, creative strivings of small children than other workers in the field, and quoting their writings more for the sake of highlighting his own unique perceptiveness than to establish the consensus on which, in the end, all scientific advances depend.

Both *The Empty Fortress* and his earlier book, *The Informed Heart*, are examples of and tributes to the human will to fight on against apparently impossible odds. Bettelheim more than once compares the struggle of the autistic child to attain identity in a family which denies his need to acquire one with that of the inmate of a concentration camp struggling to maintain his identity in a setting that is bent on destroying it. One is left in no doubt that he regards both struggles as dramatic examples of the courage we all require to maintain our autonomy and self-respect in the face of the ubiquitous depersonalizing, mechanizing forces of contemporary society – and that he would have included autistic children among the unsung heroes of our time.

Even psychoanalysis, from which he derived his main intellectual inspiration, is criticized for its failure to appreciate or respect the individuality of the infant, in its theory, and of the patient, in its practice. By conceiving of the infant as a passive creature to whom things have to be done in order to protect it from trauma and deprivation, it underestimates, Bettelheim believed, the extent to which children are, from the very beginning, active, spontaneous persons striving for recognition. And by conceiving of standard psychoanalytical technique as an end in itself, it may become a rigid procedure to which patients are subjected without reference to their particular personalities and needs. In assuming without question that psychoanalytical treatment requires a set situation to which all patients must willy-nilly conform, analysts may not only miss the opportunity of curing patients such as psychotics, for whom the setting was not designed; they may also be overriding the claims of the self and reproducing the mistake made by the patients' parents. (When Bettelheim wrote critically about psychoanalysis he always had in mind the Viennese classical psychoanalysis of his youth or the American psychoanalytical ego-psychology of his later years. He seems not to have been influenced by British object-relations theory or to have appreciated that he and Winnicott were in many ways on the same wavelength.)

In *A Home for the Heart* (1974), which Bettelheim wrote after he had ceased to be Director of the Chicago Orthogenic School, he described in meticulous detail how the School worked, what its ideals were, how its patients were treated, how its staff were selected and trained, and what role he himself as Director played in it. At a purely descriptive level the book is marvellous; it leaves the reader in no doubt that he has been presented with a true account of what really happened at the School. Regrettably, however, Bettelheim was not content just to describe how he and his staff achieved the successes they had – they claimed an 85 per cent recovery rate – but was also concerned to present his School as an example to be emulated by all other psychiatric institutions. In so doing, he largely ignored both the extent to which the School was a privileged institution and the role played in its success by his own exceptional and inimitable personality.

The privileged position enjoyed by the Orthogenic School is shown by the following facts. It never had more than fifty patients at any one time. It never had to accept a patient under a compulsory order. It never accepted patients who expressed objections to being admitted, whom it felt it could not help or who might upset patients already in residence. Patients were only accepted after having been seen by several members of the staff over a period of several days. The School selected its own staff, since many more people wanted to work there than there were posts available, and unsuitable staff were discharged and replaced easily. In fact, two-thirds of the School's therapists were asked to resign after a few months on the grounds that they were unable to meet 'the challenge to personality growth' presented by the work. The surviving third seem to have been able to satisfy Bettelheim's principle that patients should not be exposed 'to association with persons who would rather be doing something else'. Half the staff were single, lived in the School, regarded it as their home and worked a seven-day week. Both patients and staff were, in fact, highly selected. I imagine that many psychiatric institutions would have an 85 per cent recovery rate if their directors could pick and choose both their patients and their staff, instead of having to take what comes their way.

It is also clear that the School's success was largely due to Bettelheim's strong personality. Although he claimed that he granted both his staff and his patients complete autonomy, it is clear that he dominated and controlled every aspect of the School's life, and that in his own mind he and the School were identical. When a social anthropologist investigated the School he described it as a 'system of simple undifferentiated subordination', which was presumably a polite way of saying that everyone was controlled by the Director but was otherwise free to act on his own initiative. But in Bettelheim's view he created a system of 'social solidarity', by which he clearly meant what headmasters of English public schools call 'team spirit'. Indeed, he would, I am sure, have felt at home among the great reforming nineteenth-century headmasters. (Personally, I found uncanny his resemblance to Thring of Uppingham as described by Alicia C. Perceval in *Very Superior Men*, 1973.) He demanded absolute loyalty from his staff, but respected those who on occasion stood up to him – and in his own mind he was always right.

Although Bettelheim wrapped his ideas up in the most dreadful psychoanalytical jargon, his views on the origin of psychotic illness were basically very simple. Psychotics have, he believed, been subjected to indignities from the very beginning of their lives and trust no one. They can, however, learn to trust others if they are consistently treated with dignity, though it may take years to persuade them that the respect accorded to them by their therapists is sincere. Until they have learned trust they should be allowed total freedom to express their distrust and hostility, and be free to soil, hit and bite their therapists without fear of retaliation – therapists who struck a patient even once were asked to leave immediately. Only those who have had similar experiences of being subjected to indignities – Bettelheim had his when interned in a Nazi concentration camp – but have not broken down under them can treat psychotics, since only they can both understand their patients' rages and delusions and retain their equanimity. Treatment of the psychoses is treatment for both therapist and patient.

1967

1974

1990

12

Szasz and the Myth of Mental Illness

Although this started life as a discussion of just one of Thomas Szasz's books, *Ideology and Insanity*,* it emerged as a general statement of Szasz's position – and indeed of my own – on the question whether mental illnesses are truly illnesses in the medical sense or not. My own answer to this question is to be found in the essay 'Causes and Meaning' in *Psychoanalysis and Beyond*.

In 1961 Professor Szasz, an American psychoanalyst and psychiatrist, published a book entitled *The Myth of Mental Illness*. His central thesis was that there is a fallacy in supposing, as psychoanalysts and psychiatrists almost universally do, that the neuroses – and possibly many of the psychoses – are illnesses in the sense that, say, pneumonia and sciatica are, since their symptoms are not the effects of preceding causes (e.g. infection, trauma) but are active attempts to resolve apparently insoluble emotional conflicts and to communicate inadmissible thoughts and feelings. In Szasz's view, Freud's revolutionary discovery was not that hysteria is an illness with causes that can be discovered, but that hysterical symptoms are gestures and communications whose meaning can be interpreted. As a result, he argues, psychoanalysts are deceiving both themselves and their patients by claiming to treat illnesses, when they are really experts in the elucidation of the meaning of behaviour and in the resolution of emotional conflicts. In other words, psychoanalysts are flying under the wrong flag in maintaining that

* Thomas S. Szasz, *Ideology and Insanity* (London, Calder & Boyars, 1973).

psychoanalysis is a natural science and a medical specialty, when it is really one of the humanities or moral sciences.

It so happens that a small number of English analysts, notably H. J. Home but also myself, reached a rather similar conclusion by a rather different route, apparently independently of Szasz, but the thesis as propounded by Szasz in 1961 raises two difficult questions. First, is the myth of mental illness a harmless and perhaps even useful fiction, which enables persons suffering from neurotic symptoms to receive more understanding and more humane treatment than would otherwise be available to them, or a dangerous myth with consequences harmful both to patients individually and to society at large? And secondly, since the two commonest neurotic symptoms, anxiety and depression, are both bodily experiences, can neurotic behaviour really be explained and interpreted by purely psychological and social theories like Szasz's, which take no account whatsoever of biology?

I have myself come down on the side of maintaining that the myth of mental illness is a useful fiction and that Szasz's attempt to formulate a purely psychosocial theory of psychoanalysis is misguided. Szasz, on the other hand, has come down forcibly and indeed intemperately on the other side of the fence, maintaining that the myth of mental illness is a vicious idea which leads to mystification, exploitation and oppression of the so-called 'mentally ill', affords theoretical justification for trends in American society that are authoritarian, collectivist and anti-democratic, and is in any case an inherent affront to the dignity of man, since the mere act of diagnosing a person as ill disauthenticates his behaviour, attaches a stigma to him, and puts the diagnosing authority in a position of power over his victim-patient. As a result Szasz holds that, with one exception, the relationship between a psychiatrist and his patient is analogous to that between a slave-owner and a slave, an inquisitor and a witch, a jailer and a prisoner.

Szasz's one exception is the relationship between a psycho-analyst in private practice and his fee-paying patient, which, so he believes, is a free contract between equals in which power plays no part. Despite occasional statements which might lead one to believe that he is arguing the Marcusan thesis that psychiatry is a technique by which capitalism in its latest phase deludes its potential opponents into submission by persuading them that they are sick, Szasz is in fact a mid-Victorian rugged individualist, a belated believer in the Great American Dream, who views the State as an inherent enemy of human freedom. He is also, I think, a sentimentalist about private practice psychotherapy. Quite apart from the fact that differences of status and need may intrude upon the initial negotiations to fix a fee which is equitable to both patient and analyst, the analyst in private practice cannot, it seems to me, avoid at times asserting his power over his patients, since it is he, not they, who decides whether he is too ill or tired to see them, whether he is entitled to cancel sessions in order to give a lecture, attend a conference, write a book or go on holiday – and the quality of the relationship between them must therefore depend not on their equality of status but on the integrity, compassion and decency with which the analyst exercises the power which he willy-nilly has.

There are, I think, three reasons why Szasz adopted a position of such extreme antagonism towards his own profession, levelling at it charges which seem strange and bewildering to anyone whose knowledge of psychiatry and psychotherapy is confined to the way it is practised in Britain.

The first is that the American and British psychiatric scenes are in fact very different. According to Szasz – and I see no reason to disbelieve him – the following statements, not one of which could be asserted of British psychiatry, are true of America. The medical profession enjoys high prestige in society at large, and psychiatrists enjoy high prestige within the medical profession; psychoanalysts are always medically qualified and enjoy high prestige within the psychiatric fraternity; psychiatric teaching in medical schools is more intensive than students who are not going to become psychiatrists require, and is controlled either by the local psychoanalytic institute or community mental health services. Community mental health services have virtually unlimited funds at their disposal, and psychiatrists working within them have a personal financial interest in their expansion; 90 per cent of patients in mental hospitals are confined on compulsory orders – for England and Wales the comparable figure in the 1970s, the period covered by *Ideology and Insanity*, appears to have been between 5 and 10 per cent, though I suspect that both the American and the English figures should be taken with a pinch of salt.

Secondly, Szasz is an advocate of games theory, according to which society consists not of members who perform functions, nor of individuals actuated by drives, but of potentially autonomous isolates who play roles and whose behaviour is determined by the rules of the game in which they are voluntarily or involuntarily participating. In other words, society is like a repertory company, some members of which can choose the roles they play, while others have roles thrust upon them. As readers of Erving Goffman's *The Presentation of Self in Everyday Life* will know, this view of society creates insoluble problems about the nature of the self and is incapable of distinguishing between occasions when people are being themselves and when they are impersonating someone else.

By applying games theory to medicine, Szasz assumes that doctors are not persons who perform the *function* of curing and caring for those who are incapable of functioning either to their own or others' satisfaction, but are persons who have voluntarily adopted the *role* of dealing with another class of persons who have involuntarily adopted or been designated as patients. It is this idea that doctors and patients are players of roles – one role having been assumed voluntarily, the other involuntarily – which enables Szasz to assume that psychiatrists are oppressors of their patients and to compare them with slave-owners, inquisitors and jailers. The falsity of this analogy is, however, shown by the fact that Szasz himself asserts that a precondition of anyone being designated mentally ill is that he is 'inept' in either his personal or social roles. But if the mentally ill are inept, they cannot be likened to either slaves, witches or criminals; slaves, after all, had a cash value derived from their competence to work, witches were persecuted because they were believed, and sometimes claimed, to possess supernormal powers, while criminals do commit crimes – though those who get caught can arguably be described as inept.

Thirdly, Szasz is an ideologist in the worst sense of the word, a person who refuses to have any truck with the inherent untidiness of reality and is prepared to run a good idea to death for the sake of logical consistency. Although this gives him a fine nose for cant and double-think, it also prevents his appreciating that all professional people in complex societies have to deal with situations that evoke divided loyalties and demand compromise, tact, integrity and diplomacy. For instance, Szasz disapproves of student mental health services on the single ground that university psychiatrists are paid by the university and not by the students. Now, although such an arrangement is, of course, liable to abuse, the idea that it is inherently wrong assumes that the interests of students and university are always opposed and never complementary, that university psychiatrists have so little security of tenure and so little moral courage that they could never fight the university establishment on behalf of their patients, and that university staffs could never acquire enough *nous* to know what information about students they are not entitled to ask their psychiatrist to divulge. Incidentally, he also assumes that there are always private psychotherapists available within easy range of university campuses and that students can always afford their fees. This is, of course, not the case in Britain.

1973

13

Berne and Games People Play

This short piece draws attention to a tragic, ironic note in Berne's work which is all too often ignored, and which is all too uncommon in the writings of American psychotherapists.

Eric Berne's *Transactional Analysis in Psychotherapy** originally appeared in the USA in 1961, the same year as the publication there of Szasz's *The Myth of Mental Illness*, but whereas Szasz's book took only one year to cross the Atlantic, it took fourteen years for Berne's to do so. The difference in the speed of travel must have been partly due to the different tone of their two titles, *The Myth of Mental Illness* sounding popular, striking and controversial, *Transactional Analysis in Psychotherapy* learned and academic. Berne's later book, *Games People Play* (1964), despite being little more than a summary of *Transactional Analysis*, also took only a year to reach England and became a best-seller in both countries, partly no doubt on account of its catchy, racy title.

Both Szasz's and Berne's books are based on an idea that was already circulating in American psychiatric and psychological journals in the 1950s. This was that neurotic behaviour within families and other groups could be explained in terms of games theory, and that neurotic behaviour could be conceived of as ploys or gambits in games played between parents and children, between spouses, and even between psychotherapists and their patients.

*Eric Berne, *Transactional Analysis in Psychotherapy* (London: Souvenir Press, 1975).

Szasz and Berne, although both exponents of the application of games theory to human behaviour, developed their ideas along very different lines. Szasz seems to have been impressed by the fact that at the end of a game one participant is deemed to have won and the other to have lost, and as a result his myth of mental illness asserts that families, and larger groups too, play games the aim of which is to defeat one set of people or get them into a losing position, where they are diagnosed neurotic or psychotic and stigmatized as mentally ill – so that all their further moves in the game of life are disauthenticated as 'symptoms'. On this view games between parents and children, between spouses, and between different sections of society, are sinister activities, conspiracies in which one set of villains (parents, spouses, psychiatrists, slave-owners, witch-hunters) manoeuvre another set of people (children, spouses, patients, slaves, witches) into becoming victims and scapegoats. An extreme version of this conspiratorial, winner–loser interpretation of games theory is the paradoxical, Erewhonian idea that society is sick and that only those who have been diagnosed mentally ill retain their pristine, innocent vision. This gambit, by which the disauthenticated turned the tables on their oppressors and the disauthenticators were disauthenticated, was adopted in the 1960s and 1970s by the counter-culture, 'the alternative society', and by anti-psychiatrists, but never – most emphatically, never – by Szasz himself.

Berne, on the other hand, seems to have been impressed by the fact that one of the aims of playing games is to keep the ball in play, so that all the players, including the eventual losers, can enjoy it while it lasts. In Berne's view of the games people play, all the players get satisfaction of some kind from playing them, but they all, winners and losers alike, lose out in the end, since games are in the last resort distractions, procrastinations, ways of postponing engagement in the real business of life, which is loving and intimacy.

Whereas Szasz's conception of games is conspiratorial and paradoxical, Berne's is tragic and ironical, since it implies that games are in principle unnecessary, except as 'preliminary engagements', but that the great majority of human beings never take the risk of discovering that there are better things to do. Berne ends *The Games People Play* by writing:

> For certain fortunate people there is something which transcends all classifications of behaviour, and that is awareness; something which rises above the programming of the past, and that is spontaneity; and something that is more rewarding than games, and that is intimacy. But all three of these may be frightening and even perilous to the unprepared. Perhaps they are better off as they are, seeking their solutions in popular techniques of social action, such as 'togetherness'. This may mean there is no hope for the human race, but there is hope for individual members of it.

Over the years I have met several people who have claimed to know *The Games People Play* inside out and who have been adept at spotting which life or marital or sex game their spouse, lover, parent or employer is playing, but who seem not to have registered its last chapter, Chapter 18, of which I have just quoted over a half. I suspect that it was not only Berne's *credo* but also a *cri de coeur*.

1975

THE CREATIVE SELF

14

Symbolism, Imagination and Biological Destiny

This is the unaltered text of a lecture I gave at All Souls College, Oxford, as one of the 1984 Chichele Lectures. It is reprinted here by permission of the Warden and Fellows, All Souls College, from *Freud and the Humanities* (1985).

I understand that the theme of this series of Chichele Lectures is 'Psychoanalysis and Its Influence on the Arts and Humanities', and I can only suppose that I owe my invitation to contribute to the series to the fact that some forty years ago I trained as a Freudian psychoanalyst, that since then I have been practising a form of therapy which other people, perhaps rightly, insist upon calling psychoanalysis, and that I have from time to time written books and articles which can be construed as either contributions to or criticisms of psychoanalysis. This uncertainty, which exists as much in my mind as in anyone else's, arises from the fact that in sober fact there is no such thing as psychoanalysis, in the sense of a clearly defined set of ideas and techniques that are universally agreed to constitute psychoanalysis, and which are held and practised by everyone who calls himself a psychoanalyst and by no one else.

If there were such a clearly defined set of psychoanalytical ideas, it would, of course, be an easy matter to locate what influence psychoanalysis has had, and still is having, on the arts and humanities, and then, perhaps, to appraise whether that influence has been beneficial or baneful, but in fact, of course, things are not like that at all. Once upon a time it may have been possible to define as psychoanalytical any idea conceived, held and propagated by Freud and his immediate circle, but now in the 1980s, seventy years after the quarrel between Freud and Jung, fifty years after the British Psycho-Analytical Society began to be influenced by Melanie Klein, whom the Viennese analysts all regarded as a dangerous heretic, and over twenty years since existential analysis began to be imported into the English-speaking world by Laing, Rollo May and others, it has become difficult if not impossible to define precisely what this psychoanalysis is that has an influence on the arts and the humanities – and also, incidentally, on journalism and advertising.

When, fifteen years ago, I was rash enough to attempt a dictionary definition of psychoanalysis, I followed usual Freudian practice in listing the Unconscious, Resistance, and Transference as its key defining concepts, but I felt it necessary to add that the general public insisted on using the word 'psychoanalysis' to embrace all Freudian, Jungian and Adlerian ideas. Today, I would add that I think that the general public has been right to extend the meaning of the word 'psychoanalysis' in this way, to ignore the differences between the various schools and to be more impressed by their similarities. The idea that much more goes on in our minds than most people most of the time are aware of, that we not uncommonly resist the emergence into consciousness of uncomfortable and disturbing ideas, and that our present relationships are profoundly influenced by past ones – this set of ideas has, as W. H. Auden pointed out really before it had happened, become 'a whole climate of opinion', a way of looking at ourselves so pervasive that anyone not influenced by it is more likely to be resisting it than oblivious of it.

This group of ideas must, I think, be regarded as having had a beneficial effect on the arts and humanities, and indeed on our general experience of living, since it adds enrichment, depth and resonances to our every perception of ourselves and others. But it must be remembered that the poem in which Auden asserted that 'To us he [Freud] is no more a person, / Now, but a whole climate of opinion' also contains the line 'If often he was wrong and at times absurd', and there are, I believe, still in circulation a number of specifically Freudian ideas which confuse rather than enlighten and which, when applied to the arts and humanities, have a diminishing, reductionist and disparaging effect. Historically speaking, these are ideas which Freud absorbed from the rationalist, medical world in which he grew up and worked. I refer here specifically to two ideas that Freud held and built into his theories, though I doubt whether he can have consistently followed either of them in his practice. These are, first, that psychoanalysis is a natural science, no different in principle from, say, physics and chemistry, and, secondly, that it is legitimate to use pathological phenomena as paradigms of normal experience.

The first idea led him to construct a model of the mind which was based on a mechanical, neuro-anatomical metaphor, in which the actions, thoughts, feelings and aspirations of real live people were conceptualized as though they were movements of energy within and between the various parts of what he called the psychic apparatus; these movements of energy being assumed to be as casually determined as are chemical reactions or the workings of a physical apparatus. It also led him to write *as though* he observed the workings of his patients' psychic apparatuses from an external, detached, objective and indeed superior position, when in fact he must have been conversing with them. I say 'as though' he was observing his patients' mental processes, since evidence derived from the memoirs of ex-patients and from his own asides shows that in fact he chatted with patients, addressed them by nicknames, sometimes complimented them on their insight, and made friends with several of them. However, the point I am trying to make here is that Freud, out of loyalty to the idea that psychoanalysis must be a natural science, constructed a language for talking about people which could not but dehumanize them – people after all aren't apparatuses – and which not only omitted but even actively excluded any conception of an agent or self who creates or generates meaningful activity. This language, when applied to writers, artists, politicians, as it is in that curious genre of writing 'pathobiography', turns out to have disastrous consequences – at the end of reading a pathobiography the reader is liable to have lost respect both for the author and for the subject. Having said this, it would be invidious for me to cite examples, but I cannot resist the temptation to mention that Freud has himself been the subject-victim of a pathobiography.

While on the subject of psychoanalytical biographies, it is perhaps worth mentioning that there is an essential difference between the relationship of an analyst to his patient and that of a biographer to his subject. This is that the patient is a voluntary participant in the therapeutic process and can reply to his analyst's interpretations, while the subject of a biography is a passive victim who cannot. An analyst and his patient may spend hundreds of hours closeted together; interaction and communication take place between them; and the analyst's ultimate criterion of the truth of his interpretations is that the patient finds them convincing – at any rate in the long run. But an entirely different state of affairs exists between the analytical biographer-critic and his subject-victim. Although the former may have unlimited access to his subject's paintings, writings, letters, and to the various memoirs, reminiscences and conventional biographies that may already have been written about him, he has no feedback from his subject himself. The interpretations the analyst-critic makes are in no sense the result of mutual endeavour, as are those that emerge at the end of a successful analysis. The analyst-critic is deprived of the critical monitoring that would have been forthcoming if his subject had really lain on his couch and been in a position to comment and answer – and answer back.

The second specifically Freudian idea which is still around and which must, I think, be considered to be having a harmful effect is that pathological phenomena can legitimately be regarded as paradigms of normal behaviour. This has led, and still leads, people to suppose, for instance, that since anxiety is often a neurotic symptom it always is and that the perfect, healthy person would never on any occasion be anxious – not even when placed in totally unfamiliar surroundings or when confronting himself with some unusually testing task. It also led Freud to believe – and, although he eventually abandoned the idea, it is, I think, still around today – that it should be possible to explain the creativeness of artists and writers by treating imaginative activity as though it were the same sort of thing as the neurotic, infantile, perverse fantasies that he was discovering in his patients. Instead of assuming, as I imagine most people educated in the arts and humanities do, that imagination is a basic human activity, faculty or function which flowers more or less fruitfully in different people and different social and cultural settings, and that neurotic fantasies are perversions, distortions and restrictions of the imagination, Freud and the early analysts had the idea that they could explain imaginative activity by treating it as though it were the same thing as, as though it were nothing more than, neurotic fantasy. As a result papers were written by Freud and others attempting to show that the artist, like the neurotic, is a daydreamer; that the artist, like the neurotic, is reacting to infantile traumata; and, later, when many analysts became interested in depression, that the artist is making reparation for the destructive fantasies with which, as a depressive, he is burdened. And since daydreaming, infantile traumata and destructive fantasies are ubiquitous, it was not difficult to find plausible examples appearing to confirm such explanations of the origin of creative, imaginative activity.

But, characteristically, such explanations confined themselves to establishing connections between the content of works of art and the artist's presumed infantile fantasies and traumata and failed to address themselves to the specifically aesthetic issues raised by imaginative activity: the nature and origin of the artist's and writer's ability to organize his imaginings into forms or patterns that feel 'right' to him and are satisfying to others; and to transmute personal experiences and private imaginings into objects of public and universal appeal.

Psychoanalysts have, it seems to me, nothing to say about these two issues, the reason being, I suspect, that analogous issues do not in fact arise in the course of analytical practice. Analysts do not have to concern themselves with the presence or absence of formal patterns in the associations, fantasies and memories recounted to them by their patients, and they are employed by their patients to relieve disabilities and inhibitions, not to dissect the subtleties of creative functioning; it seems to be generally agreed that well-functioning capacities and 'sublimations' not only do not require analysis but are also unanalysable. As a result analysts know more about why people have hang-ups and inhibitions than why they can be creative. And although analysts may spend a lot of time and energy helping their patients to find words to match their inchoate feelings, success in doing so falls far short of enabling them to universalize their personal experiences and imaginings.

It must have been considerations of this kind that led Freud to say in 1928: 'Before the problem of the creative artist, analysis must, alas, lay down its arms.' It is, however, perhaps worth considering for a moment the implications of that 'alas, lay down its arms'. It betrays, so it seems to me, an imperialist streak in Freudian thinking, which assumes that Freud and the other Founding Fathers had discovered truths of such overwhelming and novel importance that they would be able to explain everything about human nature, and that psychoanalysis was going to have pervasive and revolutionary effects on all the arts and humanities – the possibility of a creative traffic in the opposite direction being scarcely envisaged. With the years this imperialist, expansionist tendency within the pyschoanalytical movement seems to be diminishing, perhaps because professional biographers and historians have got to work on Freud and the early history of psychoanalysis and have shown that the early analysts weren't quite as original as they seem to have thought they were, and it has become apparent that psychoanalysis is itself influenced by developments in other sciences and in the arts and humanities. But, nonetheless, I should still be somewhat surprised if a psychoanalytical college were to choose as its theme for a series of lectures 'The Arts and the Humanities and Their Influence on Psychoanalysis'. But, as we shall see, such an influence there in fact is.

The last ten minutes or so must have been heavy going, so I must lighten matters by telling an anecdote which illustrates some of the points I have been making. Some thirty years ago I was attending a conference of psychoanalysts at Geneva and sought relief from the profundities of the learned papers I was listening to in the daytime by reading a detective story in the evening. The one I chose was Wilkie Collins's The Moonstone.

However, while, as I imagined, I was relaxing from the strenuous labours of the day, psychoanalytical thinking intruded itself on my reading and I became convinced that the Moonstone of the story was a Freudian symbol for the female genitals and that its theft, the crime of the story, symbolized loss of virginity. When the conference was over and I returned to London, I pursued my hunch and, not surprisingly, I discovered no evidence at all to suggest that Wilkie Collins had suffered any infantile trauma which might have left him unconsciously pre-occupied with virginity; Collins was born in 1824 and such matters are in any case only rarely documented. But I also discovered extremely convincing evidence that as an adult he had for a while at least been consciously preoccupied with virginity and defloration. Sixteen years before writing *The Moonstone* he had written another novel, *Basil*, which has as its explicit theme the defloration of a virgin wife by someone who is not her husband.

Now it may be that when Collins wrote *The Moonstone* he was still preoccupied with virginity and that the theme re-emerged in symbolic form, but maybe, on the other hand, there is something adventitious and coincidental about the resemblance between the overt theme of one novel and the presumptive covert theme of the other – and in any case nineteenth-century men must in general have been more aware of virginity as a stealable property than we are nowadays. In some odd way, then, my psychoanalytical hunch or hypothesis had been simultaneously proved and disproved. And the aes-thetics of the case were disconcerting too. *Basil*, the novel with the overt sexual theme, is dreadfully bad, while both T. S. Eliot and Dorothy Sayers regarded *The Moonstone* as the finest detective story in the English language.

From what I have said so far, it will have become apparent that I think that assessment of the influence of psychoanalysis on the arts and humanities is complicated and confused by a contradiction within psychoanalysis itself. On the one hand, it arose as a form of medical treatment which claimed to cure sick people of illnesses, and its findings were formulated in terms of a scientific model which assumed that the laws of causation applied to mental activity just as they do to physical phenomena. But, on the other hand, its data all derive from a personal relationship, albeit a very peculiar one, between two people, one in which the therapist does not, indeed cannot, just observe mental processes going on in the patient's head and then assign causes to them, but has to use his imagination to empathize with his patient's feelings and to discover the various additional concealed meanings contained in the overt text of what the patient says to him. As a result, there is a contradiction between a theory which categorizes mental events as 'phenomena' which can be observed and have causes and a practice which regards mental activity as the creations of an agent who generates meanings in everything he says and does – and who, characteristically, generates more meanings than he is, at the moment of generation, aware of.

Now, this contradiction is widely, though not universally, recognized by analysts themselves, though they speak, I think, more often of divorces, gaps and discrepancies between theory and practice than of contradictions. However, André Green, the French analyst, talks of 'confusions at the very heart of psychoanalysis', while Thomas Szasz, the American analyst, has declared mental illness to be a myth and argues that psychoanalysis is a semantic theory and should be categorized as a moral not a natural science. And Roy Schafer, another American analyst, is at present reformulating psychoanalytical theory in what he calls 'action language', based on the assumption that psychoanalysis is one of the humanities and that its central concept is *the person as agent* – an agent whose actions have meanings not causes, who does things because he has reasons for doing them not because he is impelled to do them by causes. Leaning heavily on Oxford philosophers, notably Gilbert Ryle, Schafer argues that actions do not have causes, are not propelled by forces or impulses located in the id or the ego or anywhere else, for the simple reason that the forces and structures postulated by classical Freudian theory do not in fact exist. They are merely abstract nouns, and one is guilty of the logical fallacy of reification if one adduces them as causes. Nor is there really any place or structure called the mind or the psychic apparatus within which forces, drives, instincts, ids, egos, and super-egos can be located.

Now, this 'action language' version of psychoanalysis certainly is an example of its being influenced by the humanities, and it can indeed be taken as evidence that psychoanalysis is on its way to becoming one of them. However, if it does, it will have, if it is to avoid letting a number of babies out with the bath water, to reformulate in humanistic terms a number of insights and concepts which to date have remained firmly imbedded in classical Freudian language. It was to some of these that I was referring when I lumbered this lecture with its portentous, pretentious title 'Symbolism, Imagination and Biological Destiny'.

According to classical Freudian theory there exists a class of symbols, most easily observed in dreams, which stand for bodily, mostly sexual, organs and processes, and repressed impulses achieve disguised, hallucinatory fulfilment by using these symbols to, as it were, fool the censorship imposed by the proprieties of consciousness. Furthermore, the theory holds that such Freudian symbols are constructed by movements of energy within the psychic apparatus, the two movements in question being displacement, by which energy moves from one mental image to another, and condensation, by which energy invested in more than one image is concentrated on one.

All very puzzling and difficult, and I doubt whether in a single paragraph I can have given an account of the Freudian theory of symbolism that is either accurate or fair. But the point I wish to make here is that this theory contains insights of paramount importance to the arts and humanities, though this only becomes evident after one has translated the theory out of the natural-scientific language used by Freud into, I am tempted to say, ordinary English. One can then appreciate that Freud's statements about the movements of mental energy from one image to another are really statements about how we endow and attribute meanings to the objects we perceive and construct images of, and that what psychoanalysis has discovered is that human beings, presumably unlike other animals, think, imagine and dream in metaphor, seeing similarities between their own bodies and their bodies' activities on the one hand and objects and processes perceived in the outside world on the other.

As Marion Milner in particular has pointed out, there seems to be a general, innate tendency to apprehend all objects that are not one's self by likening them to bodily organs and processes that are one's self, a tendency that enables us to assimilate the originally alien outside world into the inevitably and primordially familiar world of one's own body and its sensations, and that provides us with a stock of images which we can liken to our own bodies and activities and to which our own bodies and activities can be likened. As a result imagery derived from our own body is available for making metaphorical, symbolic statements about the outside world – and about our own mental processes – and imagery derived from the outside world is available for making metaphorical, symbolic statements about ourselves, about our physical and mental state of being. In other words, there is a two-way imaginative traffic between our own body and its activities on the one hand and objects in the outside world on the other, so that each provides metaphors to describe the other.

I have spelled out in detail elsewhere this idea that one of the most important discoveries of psychoanalysis (perhaps *the* most important) is that man is a symbolizing animal who constructs on the foundation of his elemental bodily experiences a network of images which embraces and orders all his perceptions of the outside world. This network, or rather the activity of this network, is, I conceive, what we call imagination. It enables us to do not only what all other animals can do, viz. react adaptively to the immediate present, but also to anticipate and rehearse the future, to relive the past – as Bartlett pointed out years ago, remembering is an imaginative not a reproductive activity – to conceive how it would be to be someone else, to imagine how things could be other than they are and to construct fictive alternative worlds. For the last 250 years or so, this last use of the imagination has enjoyed a special status in our society, and there are indeed people who would restrict the word 'imagination' to mean solely the capacity to create original works of art.

Finally, I must turn to the last term in my title, Biological

Destiny, and while doing so I shall draw attention to and, I hope, dispel a popular misconception about psychoanalysis that has, I think, a bad and misleading effect. This is the idea that, according to Freud, all symbols are sexual – hence, of course, the popular cant phrase 'Freudian symbol'.

Now, the statement that most symbols occurring in dreams are sexual can indeed be found in Freud's writing, but the passage in which it occurs turns out, on close inspection, to contain a category error, and once this error is eliminated Freud and psychoanalysis are revealed as saying something much more momentous than the popular idea that all dreams are sexual.

The crucial passage occurs in Freud's Tenth Introductory Lecture (1916) where he says: 'The range of things which are given symbolic representation in dreams is not wide: the human body as a whole, parents, children, brothers and sisters, birth, death, nakedness – and something else besides.' This 'something else besides' turns out to be 'the field of sexual life – the genitals, sexual processes, sexual intercourse. The great majority of symbols in dreams are sexual symbols. And here a strange disproportion is revealed. The topics I have mentioned are few, but the symbols for them are extremely numerous.' Freud then goes on to list over thirty symbols for the male genitals and over twenty for the female.

Now, reading or hearing this quotation, and indeed the whole lecture from which it is taken, it is easy to conclude that Freud thought that in sleep at least we are all obsessed by sex, but once one has spotted that there is something very peculiar about his categories, the picture changes significantly. In the first place Freud says that 'the range of things which are given symbolic representation in dreams is not wide' but then goes on to give a list of things – the body, parents, children, brothers and sisters, birth, death, nakedness, and that something else besides – which covers an extremely wide range of human experience, in fact almost everything apart from work, play and intellectual activity. And in the second place, by calling 'the field of sexual life' 'something else besides', he puts sex into a different category from the other items on his list, when in fact it has intimate connections with them all. Indeed, far from being 'something else besides', it is precisely what links all his other things symbolized together. After all, to go through Freud's list: we only have a body because our parents had sexual intercourse, at least once; we only have children because (or if) we have had sexual intercourse; we only have brothers and sisters because (or if) our parents had sexual intercourse more than once; birth and death are the first and last members of the series birth, copulation and death; and nakedness has obvious connections with sex, and birth and death.

So, if one refuses to follow Freud in his categorization of sex as something else besides, it becomes possible to reformulate his statements about symbolism in more general, inclusive terms, without in any way bowdlerizing them. It becomes possible to say that the range of things symbolized in dreams embraces all aspects of man's life-cycle, and that the psychoanalytical study of dreams reveals that human beings are more preoccupied than they mostly realize with their biological destiny – to use the widest term possible to encompass the whole life-cycle of birth, growth, love, reproduction, ageing and death. And this life-cycle has to be called destiny, however portentous the word sounds, because it is determined only marginally by conscious choices and decisions but mainly by biological patterns that are inborn and ineluctable (e.g. one's innate vitality, temperament, aptitudes, age of onset of puberty and ageing) and by social factors over which we have had no choice. We did not choose our parents or select which genes they should pass on to us, nor the culture into which we were born, nor the impact upon us of the various social, economic and intellectual movements at work within that culture.

1984

W. H. Auden, 'In Memory of Sigmund Freud' in Collected Poems, ed. Edward Mendelson (London: Faber & Faber, 1969).
Frederic Bartlett, Remembering (Cambridge: Cambridge University Press, 1932).
Sigmund Freud, 'Introductory Lectures on Psychoanalysis', in SE vol. 15 (London: The Hogarth Press, 1963).
    'Dostoevsky and Parricide', in SE vol. 21 (London: The Hogarth Press, 1961).

André Green, quoted by Peter Fuller in 'A Chat of Analysts', *New Society*, 31 July 1975.
R. D. Laing, *The Divided Self* (London: Tavistock, 1960).
The Self and Others (London: Tavistock, 1960).
Rollo May, *Psychology and the Human Dilemma* (New York: Norton, 1979).
Marion Miller, 'Aspects of Symbolism in Comprehension of the Not-Self', *International Journal of Psychoanalysis*, vol. 33 (1952).
Charles Rycroft, 'The Analysis of a Detective Story' in *Imagination and Reality* (London: The Hogarth Press, 1968).
   A Critical Dictionary of Psychoanalysis (London: Nelson, 1968; Harmondsworth: Penguin Books, 1972).
   The Innocence of Dreams (London: The Hogarth Press, 1979, 1991).
Roy Schafer, *A New Language for Psychoanalysis* (New Haven and London: Yale University Press, 1976).
Max Schur, *Freud: Living and Dying* (London: The Hogarth Press, 1972).
Thomas Szasz, *The Myth of Mental Illness* (London: Secker & Warburg, 1962).

15

Remembering, Imagining, Creating

This lecture was given on 7 March 1987 at Mapperley Hospital, Nottingham, to a symposium on Creativity and Psychotherapy.

It is always a good thing to begin at the beginning, so I shall start this lecture by quoting the first one and a half verses of the first chapter of the First Book of Moses, called Genesis: 'In the beginning God created the heaven and the earth. And the earth was without form, and void.' My reason for doing so is to draw attention to the fact that there is a deep ambiguity imbedded in the concept of creativeness. Does it refer to the process of making something out of nothing, in which case the object created would be *absolutely* novel and original, or to the process of creating order out of chaos, of restructuring, transforming and developing elements and items already in existence to create something only *relatively* novel and original?

The *Shorter Oxford English Dictionary*, always a great standby in times of trouble, gives the former as the primary meaning of 'to create', citing in its favour Dr Johnson's dictionary definition 'to form out of nothing', and prefacing the entry with the words 'Said of God'. But it also quotes a Victorian Dean of St Paul's, Henry Longueville Mansel, as saying, 'We can think of creation only as a change in the condition of that which already exists.'

Now, although the point, the distinction, I have just been making may sound pedantic, there are, I think, two reasons for supposing it to be of some slight importance. First, there have been, and probably still are, religious people who consider that the claim of writers, painters, composers, thinkers, etc., to be creative is offensive, arrogant, presumptuous and blasphemous; and there must be many people – I am one of them myself – who don't feel quite happy about such notions as creative advertising, creative salesmanship, creative cooking. It would seem that activities only qualify for the designation 'creative' if they are not entirely earthbound and this-worldly and if they display some quality which is more than lively, intelligent and inventive.

Secondly, psychotherapists do on occasion encounter patients who claim to be creative and whose claim is indeed the arrogant one that they will be able to create something absolutely *de novo* without indebtedness to anyone else. I have described such people in a paper I wrote some years ago and entitled 'On Ablation of the Parental Images, or The Illusion of Having Created Oneself'. In it I suggested that there exists a class of persons who have an urgent need to repudiate their biological and cultural ancestry, who claim to be self-created, self-made men (and just occasionally women) indebted in no way to anyone else. Such people do, it seems to me, believe that it is possible to create something out of nothing. They are not content to believe that their creativeness consists in an ability to restructure and transform what they have acquired from parents, teachers, predecessors and from the intellectual, aesthetic and moral climate in which they have grown up. The psychoanalytical word for such people is omnipotent, a term which is, of course, borrowed from religion, where it applies only to God.

If, however, we discard the idea that creativeness is the ability to make something out of nothing, and accept that it must be the ability to create order out of chaos, and to develop and trans-form elements already in existence, two things seem to follow. First, it must be possible to relate any individual person's creativeness to a whole number of sources *external* to himself, to such sources as his genetic endowment, his relationships with his parents and siblings, his education, the social and cultural climate in which he spent his formative years. There must, indeed, be a sense in which all individual creativeness is also society's creativeness.

People sometimes talk as though geniuses are exceptions to

the idea that creativeness is contingent on milieu, but surely Leonardo da Vinci, Newton and Beethoven would all have remained mute, inglorious Miltons if there had been no demand for paintings – and no apprenticeship system for promising painters – in Renaissance Italy, if there had been no scientific revolution, and no dons at Trinity College, Cambridge, teaching mathematics in the seventeenth century, if there had been no demand for music and no patronage of musicians in the eighteenth century. I say this because I think that as psychotherapists we are too inclined to think of creativeness solely in terms of individual psychopathology and to ignore the social setting which enables it to develop or prevents it from doing so.

Secondly, it must be possible to relate the details of any creative product to ideas, images, concepts that were already present in its creator's mind before he created it. In other words, creating must be a function of a form of remembering.

In the days when creative people protected themselves against the risk of being accused of arrogance and hubris by claiming that they were inspired by a Muse, whose mere vessel they were, they also believed that their particular muse was one of the nine daughters of Mnemosyne, the goddess of memory. Mnemosyne, incidentally, was herself the daughter of Uranus and Gaea, of Heaven and Earth. Here we have, I think, a statement, albeit in mythological and archaic terms, of something that I mentioned earlier on, that activity only qualifies for the designation 'creative' if it has some quality that raises it above the earthbound and on to some 'higher' level. What this quality is, and how the creative person generates it, is, of course, the great mystery; it has, I presume, something to do with the form that the creative person imposes on the mnemic material as it emerges, and with the presence within that form of more themes, more meanings, more resonances than are immediately apparent.

Anyone who doubts that the elements of any creative product, of any work of art, derive from memory, and that creating is a kind of remembering should read John Livingstone Lowes' *The Road to Xanadu*, in which he demonstrates that the details of 'Kubla Khan' derive almost exclusively from travel books that Coleridge had read. But Coleridge's imagination has transformed and combined these details to construct a place that no one other than the poet has ever visited.

The relationship of creative activity to remembering, and the way in which it transforms images derived from perceptions into something which is in some way less earthbound, is described by Wordsworth in a passage from the Preface to *Lyrical Ballads* which most of us know in the truncated, condensed and incorrect form: Poetry is emotion remembered in tranquillity. The full text is, however, more illuminating:

> Poetry takes its origins from emotion remembered in tranquillity. The emotion is contemplated till, by a species of reaction, the tranquillity gradually disappears, and an emotion kindred to that which was before the object of contemplation, is gradually produced, and does itself actually exist in the mind.

The obscurity of this passage, and the mystery that still surrounds creativeness, is concentrated in the idea that 'by a species of reaction' 'an emotion kindred to' the one remembered is engendered during the creative activity of poetic composition. Psychoanalytical theory has attempted to explain this 'species of reaction' by invoking the concept of sublimation, that process by which the emotions attached to drives, images and memories can undergo transformation, elevating them to a 'higher' level; but it has, I think, not been altogether successful in defining or even describing the true quality of transformed, sublimated affects. It tends to do so in solely negative terms, describing them as neutralized, de-aggressified and de-libidinized.

Wordsworth's insight into the fact that creative activity is a matter of transforming memories presumably came to him because he was an introspective, contemplative man who devoted much of his life to meditating on the origins of his own poetic gifts. His most famous poem, *The Prelude*, was indeed described by himself as 'the poem on the growth of my own mind'. Less reflective, less self-absorbed writers may, however, be surprised at discovering how closely intertwined creating and remembering are. Mary Lavin, the Irish writer, speaking on the Dublin radio, remarked: 'I recognize details from my life in my stories that I could never remember at will – a flower, the river, a landscape. The details themselves don't interest me very much, because I accept that involuntary memory is a part of creativity, but I am interested in why one remembers meaningless things.' As psychotherapists we would, I think, be inclined to doubt whether things remembered ever are meaningless since we are familiar with the return of previously unremembered memories in our patients' – and indeed our own – nocturnal creations, dreams.

I have been speaking of creating and remembering and have so far only once found it necessary to refer to the third item in my title, imagining. This was when I attributed the transformation of Coleridge's reading matter into the poem 'Kubla Khan' to Coleridge's imagination. But what is imagination? Is it some peculiar, mysterious, undefinable faculty that imaginative, creative people happen to have, and unimaginative people lack? Or is it a faculty that we all have, that plays an essential part in everyone's life, and is amenable to description and definition? The latter is, I think and hope, the case.

For definitions I turn again to the *Shorter Oxford English Dictionary*, which gives three non-obsolete ones. First, imagination is 'the action of imagining, or forming a mental concept of what is not actually present to the senses'. Secondly, it is 'that faculty of the mind by which we conceive the absent as if it were present'. And thirdly, 'it is the *power* which the mind has of forming concepts beyond those derived from external objects'.

Now, the first two definitions link imagination and memory, imagining and remembering, and memory has indeed been called 'reproductive imagination'. According to Frederic Bartlett – I quote from his classic *Remembering* (1932) – 'Remembering is not the re-excitation of innumerable fixed, lifeless and fragmentary traces. It is an imaginative reconstruction, or construction, built out of the relation of our (present) attitude towards a whole active mass of organized past reactions or experience.' In other words, remembering is not the mechanical retrieval of fixed items from a memory store, which is separate from the rest of our mind, but an imaginative dialectic between our present self and our past experience, both of which are active and lively. Not only may we wish to remember the past, the past may wish to be remembered.

This view of memory as a function of imagination, and remembering as a kind of imagining, accords well with psycho-analytical theory with its emphasis on the pervasive role of unconscious fantasy, even though Freud himself seems to have subscribed to the idea that memory is a store from which items can be retrieved and from which items at times erupt.

The third dictionary definition, that imagination is the power which the mind has of forming concepts beyond those derived from external objects, is obviously the one which has most bearing on creativeness. Unless, as I mentioned earlier, one is prepared to believe in the possibility of creating something out of nothing, forming concepts, images, etc., *beyond* those derived from external objects must in fact be a matter of fragmenting images, percepts and concepts derived from external objects and then recombining the resulting fragments to form novel images and patterns. Freud used the terms 'displacement', 'conden-sation' and 'symbolization' to describe the way in which images derived from the recent past (day's residue) and from the remote past (infantile memories) are reshuffled and then coalesce to form dreams, while Coleridge, who like Wordsworth took a psychologist's interest in his own creative processes, said that imagination 'dissolves, diffuses, dissipates, in order to recreate'.

One remarkable thing about the imagination is that it is independent of the will. As a result its products are likely to surprise its owner. Although when awake we can by an act of will make ourselves do things, learn things, think about things, we can only let ourselves imagine and we may be surprised by what we find ourselves imagining. And asleep we cannot make ourselves do anything, even dream; we just do on occasion dream, and even the most experienced analysand or analyst continues to be surprised by his dreams.

This point, and others, was well made by Charles Darwin who, over twenty years before the publication of Freud's *The Interpretation of Dreams*, wrote:

The Imagination is one of the highest prerogatives of man. By this faculty he unites former images and ideas, independently of the will, and thus creates brilliant and novel results. A poet, as Jean Paul Richter remarks, 'who must reflect whether he shall make a character say yes or no – to the devil with him; he is only a stupid corpse.' Dreaming gives us the best notion of this power; as Jean Paul again says 'The dream is an involuntary kind of poetry.'

Having made this point, that imaginative activity is independent of the will, it is necessary to make two glosses on it. First, a lot of art that purports to be creative and imaginative is in fact willed; critics call such works contrived, fanciful or *voulu*, terms which imply that the work in question is somehow not quite the real thing.

Secondly, some people have the gift, acquire the art, learn the knack, of being able to be receptive to their own imaginative capacity. When this happens, a happy dialectic can take place between two parts of the personality that are all too often opposed to one another, and the individual, while creating, becomes simultaneously active and passive, assertive and receptive, imaginative and realistic, elevated and earthbound. But this happy conjunction can only occur, it seems to me, in people who are prepared to wait a little while for their muse to visit them, and who don't shout too loudly when they call spirits from the vasty deep.

1987

Frederic Bartlett, *Remembering* (Cambridge: Cambridge University Press, 1932).

Charles Darwin, *The Descent of Man*, 2 vols (London: John Murray, 1871).

Sigmund Freud, 'The Interpretation of Dreams' (1900), in *Standard Edition*, vols 4 and 5 (London: The Hogarth Press, 1953).

John Livingstone Lowes, *The Road to Xanadu* (Boston: Houghton Mifflin, 1927).

John Quinn (ed.), *A Portrait of the Artist as a Young Girl* (London: Methuen, 1986).

Charles Rycroft, 'On Ablation of the Parental Images', in *Psychoanalysis and Beyond* (London: The Hogarth Press, 1985).

16

Look Back in Loathing

As the reader will discover, this review of Sartre's *Words*,* written over twenty-five years ago, turns out to exemplify some of the points I will make in the most recent, and final, piece in this book, 'On Selfhood and Self-Awareness'.

Although Sartre's *Words* was described on the dustcover as 'reminiscences' and 'the first volume of his autobiography', its interest lies largely in the way in which it does not conform to the genre – or rather, in the fact that its *raison d'être* differs from that of most autobiographies. Sartre's motive for describing his childhood – this volume leaves him in his early teens – was certainly not to evoke it for its own sake, since he says, 'I loathe my childhood and all that remains of it'; nor was it to unburden himself of a compulsive recollecting of it, since he confesses to having found it hard to recapture and to having a general tendency to erase and disown his past; nor was it to satisfy the curiosity of his admirers; nor even to make a Confession or Exhibition, though this does come into it a little; but rather to describe his recovery from what can variously be called a psychosis, an illusion or a fallacy. And one cannot but surmise that the writing formed part of the recovery.

The fallacy from which Sartre records his recovery was Platonic idealism, the theory that it is ideas and words that are real and that the objective world only exists to exemplify and incarnate them.

* Jean-Paul Sartre, *Words* (London: Hamish Hamilton, 1964).

A Platonist by condition, I moved from knowledge to its object; I found ideas more real than things, because they were the first to give themselves to me and because they gave themselves like things. I met the universe in books; assimilated, classified, labelled and studied, but still impressive; and I confused the chaos of my experiences through books with the hazardous course of real events. Hence my idealism which it took me thirty years to undo.

I never scratched the soil or searched for nests; I never looked for plants or threw stones at birds. But books were my birds and my nests, my pets, my stable and my countryside; the library was the world trapped in a mirror.

The psychological problem which besets the idealist is how to derive his own identity, which can only stem from his being an idea in someone else's mind. 'Seen, I saw myself; I saw myself reading as one hears oneself speak.' Sartre was brought up in a family in which God had insufficient vitality to provide the basis of his own sense of being, and so he had to find substitutes for the Great Spectator demanded by idealism. And some of the more obvious ones were also missing in Sartre's childhood:

A father would have ballasted me with a few lasting prejudices; . . . he would have dwelt in me; this respectable tenant would have given me self-respect. I would have based my right to live on this respect. My begetter would have decided on my future: destined from birth to be an engineer, I should have been reassured for life.

But his father had died when he was a few months old. An only child, he was brought up by his maternal grandparents, who referred to him and his mother as 'the children' and who rarely mentioned his father.

Nor was his own body a source of reality.

This would have been fine if I had got on all right with my body. But it and myself formed an odd couple. A poor child does not question itself; ravaged *bodily* by want and sickness, its unjustifiable condition justifies its existence. Hunger and the constant danger of death are the bases of its right to live: it lives so as not to die. But I was not rich enough to consider myself predestined nor poor enough for my envious wishes to be exigent. I fulfilled my alimentary duties and God sometimes – rarely – sent me that grace which permits you to eat without disgust – appetite.

So Sartre, uninhabited by his father and alienated from his own body, had no choice but to incarnate his mother's and –

more particularly – his grandfather's illusions. When at their instigation he realized that he was destined to be a Writer, to invoke Humanity as the Spectator in front of whom he could play the roles of Priest, Hero and Saviour, he said,

I unloaded onto the writer the consecrated powers of the hero. The clergy [i.e. the intelligentsia, *les clercs*] took charge of humanity and saved it by the reversibility of merits; the wild beasts of the temporal world, great and small, had ample leisure in which to kill each other or to lead a dazed and truthless existence since writers and artists meditated on their behalf on Beauty and Goodness. To tear the entire human race from its animal state, only two conditions were required; that the relics of dead clerics – paintings, books, statues – should be preserved in supervised premises; and that at least one living cleric should remain to carry on the task and manufacture future relics.

This 'squalid nonsense', as the later disillusioned Sartre was to call it, derived from his grandfather, Karl or Charles Schweitzer, a teacher who regarded literature as a museum of which he was the curator. 'I swallowed it down without really understanding it, and I still believed it at twenty.'

Although Sartre derived his dedication as a writer from his grandfather's and mother's idealization of him, the story has an ironic twist in it. Although he was spoiled by them, regarded as 'a present from heaven' and an infant prodigy, and was, for instance, removed from his first school because the headmaster failed to endorse his genius, his canonization of himself as a Writer, who could create his own world, was not due to their direct encouragement but was his response to the humiliating discovery that it was not enough to play the parts they cast him in. They, he eventually realized, could exist without Him, and he had a walking-on part not a Lead in the Comedy they played.

My true self, my character and my name were in the hands of adults; I had learnt to see myself through their eyes . . . The worst of it was that I suspected the grown-ups of play-acting. The words they spoke to me were like sweets; but they talked to each other in a very different way . . . I would have on my most adorable pout, the one of which I was surest, and they would say in genuine tones 'Go and play over there, Child, we're talking.' . . . Since no one claimed me *seriously*, I set up the pretension that I was indispensable to the universe . . . To escape the desolation of created things, I prepared for myself the middle-class solitude for which there is no cure: that of the creator . . . I was born from writing: before that there was only a reflexion in a mirror . . . By writing I existed, I escaped from the grown-ups.

So to rescue himself from one illusion he created another, and by a further twist this was simultaneously undermined and reinforced by his grandfather who, aghast at the prospect of his darling really becoming a serious writer – do not such people become drunkards and sometimes die of hunger? – instructed him to become a teacher who wrote as a sideline.

With well placed little touches, Charles persuaded me that I was not a genius . . . Lost, I accepted, in obedience to Karl, the dedicated career of a minor writer. In short, he flung me into literature by the pains he took to steer me away from it: to the extent that sometimes even today when I am in a bad mood, I ask myself if I have not used up so many days and nights, covered so many sheets of paper with my ink, dumped on the market so many books that no one wanted, in the sole mad hope of pleasing my grandfather.

But why did his grandfather's injunction take? 'Why did I pay attention to [his voice] that very day when it was telling the most deliberate lies? . . . It was the voice that had changed; it was dry and hard and I took it for that of the absentee who had begotten me.'

So after all a father did ballast him with a few lasting prejudices and dwell in him, and he acquired an identity and a future, but at the price of both impediments and illusions. The impediments have not been lost – 'My commandments have been sewn into my skin: if I go a day without writing, the scar burns me, and if I write too easily, it also burns me – but the illusions have been.' Or have they?

My retrospective illusions are in pieces. Martyrdom, salvation, immortality: all are crumbling; the building is falling in ruins. I have caught the Holy Ghost in the cellars and flung him out of them. Atheism is a cruel, long-term business: I believe I have gone through it to the end. I see clearly. I am free from illusions. I know my real tasks, and I must surely deserve a civic prize; for about ten years I have been a man who is waking up, cured of a long, bitter-sweet madness, who cannot get away from it, who cannot recall his old ways without laughing and who no longer has any idea what to do with his life . . . I have renounced my vocation but I have not unfrocked myself. I still write. What else can I do?

1964

17

Sartre's Vision of Freud

The Freud Scenario by Jean-Paul Sartre* contains the texts of the two scripts that Sartre wrote for John Huston's film *Freud, The Secret Passion*. (In view of the fact that Anna Freud raised objections to the suggestion that Marilyn Monroe should play the female lead in the film, it is interesting to note that in the 1970s the Hampstead Child Therapy Clinic, of which Anna Freud was founder and Director, received 'a sizeable portion of the tardily settled estate of Marilyn Monroe'. Monroe had left money to her first analyst, Marianne Kris, with instructions that she should give it to a charity of her choice. See Elisabeth Young-Bruehl's *Anna Freud: A Biography*, 1989.)

In 1958 John Huston, the American film director, invited Jean-Paul Sartre to write the script for a film on Freud. Huston's idea was, apparently, that the film should concentrate on the 'heroic' period of Freud's life, when he abandoned hypnosis for free association, and the traumatic, seduction theory of neurosis for the Oedipus complex and dream interpretation, and that Sartre would be the ideal man to write the screenplay since 'he knew Freud's works intimately and would have an objective and rational approach'. Readers of J.-B. Pontalis's preface to the present work will, however, have doubts as to whether Huston can really have had any idea of what kind of film he wanted to make or, indeed, how much he knew about Freud when he conceived the idea of making a film about him, or whether he

---

*Jean-Paul Sartre, *The Freud Scenario*, ed. J.-B. Pontalis (London: Verso, 1986).

had any grounds for supposing that Sartre had an intimate knowledge of Freud's work or an objective and rational approach towards him.

Sartre accepted Huston's commission, and the fee, which was apparently a large one, and set to work. In 1959 he handed in a script for a film which would have run for at least seven hours, and then, when asked to revise and cut it, rewrote it extensively but lengthened it. At some point Huston got fed up with Sartre – and, presumably, Sartre got fed up with Huston – and the two Sartre scripts were handed over to two professional script-writers, Charles Kaufmann and Wolfgang Reinhardt, who used them to write the script for the film that Huston eventually made, *Freud, The Secret Passion*. Sartre refused to allow his name to appear in the credits and probably never bothered to see the film, while Huston's autobiography is apparently bitter about Sartre. Both Sartre and Huston have left accounts of the weeks they spent together in Huston's country house in Ireland: according to Sartre, 'Huston shuns thought because it makes him sad'; according to Huston, 'there was no such thing as conversation with him . . . there was no interrupting him . . . the drone of his voice followed me until I was out of earshot and, when I'd return, he wouldn't even have noticed that I'd been gone'.

The Freud Scenario, edited by J.-B. Pontalis, the well-known French psychoanalyst, contains the full text of Sartre's first script, extracts from his second script, Sartre's own synopsis of his first script, and a table collating the two scripts. Of these four items only the first will be of interest to the general reader, since it must presumably give a true picture of the vision of Freud and psychoanalysis that Sartre created for himself before he had been confronted by the exigencies of Huston's personality and the realities of the American film industry.

Although some reviewers of *The Freud Scenario* have dismissed it as kitsch, I found it, I must confess, a good read. Once I had reconciled myself to the fact that it has no pretensions to historical accuracy but is an attempt to give a dramatic, visual presentation of a crisis in medical history and in Freud's own personal development, I was impressed by the insight it shows into the fantasy life of hysterical patients, into the bafflement suffered by well-meaning, unimaginative physicians when confronted by hysterical behaviour, and into the agonies Freud endured before he reconciled himself to the fact that he was a born loner who could not go through life uncritically revering his actual father and attaching himself to a series of father-figures (Meynert, Breuer, Fliess).

This last relationship is, indeed, the central theme of *The Freud Scenario*. As Pontalis points out, Sartre, who in effect never had a father and did not think much of fatherhood – 'The rule is that there are no good fathers; it is not the men who are at fault, but the paternal bond which is rotten' – was fascinated by Freud's compulsion to attach himself to father-figures and then with much agonizing to extricate himself from their toils, and by his eventual achievement of a most remarkable state of solitude and independence. In the last scene of the Scenario Sartre has Freud standing by his father's grave saying, 'He's dead. And my adoptive fathers are buried with him. I'm alone face to face with myself and I no longer hate anyone . . . I'm alone and the sky has emptied. I'll work alone, I'll be my sole judge and my sole witness.' It is, of course, most unlikely that Freud ever said anything of the kind, but he did once write, in a letter to Ferenczi: 'I no longer have any need to uncover my personality completely . . . I have succeeded where the paranoiac fails.'

One remarkable thing about *The Freud Scenario* is that Sartre wrote it before most of the sources on which we now rely for our understanding of Freud and the origins of psychoanalysis became available. In fact, Sartre seems only to have used three source books: the first volume of Jones's life of Freud, which had just been translated into French; the selection of Freud's letters to the Berlin ear, nose and throat specialist, Wilhelm Fliess, the French translation of which had appeared two years earlier; and Freud and Breuer's *Studies on Hysteria*, which provided him with the clinical details from which he constructed his heroine, if that is the right word. This hysterical lady's interactions with Freud and Breuer provide the drama of the text and convince Freud that he and his patients have not actually been seduced by their fathers but have been in the thrall of the Oedipus complex.

Either Huston or Sartre – Pontalis and the English translator disagree on this point – wanted Marilyn Monroe to play this part, but Anna Freud objected, and in the event it was played by Susannah York. In addition to these three source books, Sartre also culled a number of Freud's own dreams from *The Interpretation of Dreams*.

According to Pontalis, 'serious or peevish minds – and these are often one and the same – will conclude that his research work was neither very extensive nor very meticulous', but personally I am struck by the fact that Sartre seems to have divined the full intensity of Freud's dependence on Fliess without having read *The Complete Letters of Sigmund Freud to Wilhelm Fliess*. These were only released in 1984, and so Sartre did not know that Freud allowed Fliess to operate on the noses of himself and his patients and on one now notorious occasion preferred to deceive himself grossly rather than admit to himself that Fliess had been professionally negligent. Sartre could not, either, have read Henri F. Ellenberger's *The Discovery of the Unconscious* (1970), in which Freud's self-analysis and elaboration of psychoanalysis are seen as manifestations of a creative illness: I am impressed by the clarity with which Sartre, without any of these sources, saw so clearly the intimate connection between Freud's creativeness and his neurosis.

1986

18

Rousseau: Man and Superwoman

This short account of Jean Guéhenno's *Jean-Jacques Rousseau,** is also, one could say, a study in the pathology of self-awareness.

Few men can have more to answer for than Rousseau. The Romantic movement, the autobiographical novel in which the author gazes nostalgically and lovingly at his innocent childhood self, the political theories and revolutions based on the flattering but undemonstrable, and perhaps even meaningless, assertion that Man is born good, equal and free, the idea that a People is a real entity with a Will and a Destiny that can override that of the individuals who compose it – all these derive more or less directly from Rousseau's *La Nouvelle Héloïse, Confessions* and *The Social Contract*, and they all display the inflation of self and the contempt for facts which characterized Rousseau's own personality.

M. Jean Guéhenno's two volumes, which first appeared in French in 1948 and 1952 and were published in England in 1966, are neither a biography nor a critical study but rather a record of the author's attempt to live with Rousseau and to discover to what extent the author of the *Confessions* really was the person he presented himself as being:

> More than once, I have felt that Jean-Jacques was sitting opposite me, a great, ranting, marvellously eloquent ghost, and so sincere that I could not but feel ridiculous as his opponent in the kind of game we were playing, which was the contest for truth. I picked holes in his state-

* Jean Guéhenno's, *Jean-Jacques Rousseau*, translated by John and Doreen Weightman, 2 vols (London: Routledge & Kegan Paul, 1966).

ments, produced my petty proofs, pushed forward my little bits of paper. 'You are mistaken,' I would murmur, 'here, and here again. I am not suggesting that you are actually telling lies, but you certainly know how to cover up. You do so unconsciously.'

For anyone who has not been brought up to regard Rousseau as a hero, it is indeed extremely difficult not to dismiss him as a humbug and a liar. Difficult too not to regard his *Confessions*, not as a work of supreme honesty, but as a masterpiece of rationalizing self-justification, despite their proud opening boast:

I have resolved upon an undertaking which is without precedent and will find no imitator. I wish to reveal to my fellow-creatures a man in the utter truth of his nature. And this man will be myself. Myself alone. I understand my own heart . . .

M. Guéhenno himself seems to think that Rousseau's need to justify himself in the eyes of both posterity and God derived mainly from his remorse at having got rid of his five children by depositing them in a foundling hospital. He cites more than one instance of Rousseau's confessing to this outrage, then justifying it dramatically:

Nevertheless I render thanks to Heaven for having inflicted the bitter experiences of life only on me, while sparing my children. I would rather they led an obscure and humble life without knowing me . . . My position is without parallel; there has never been another case like mine since the world began . . . I AM INNOCENT.

But it seems that Rousseau had another reason for needing to justify himself. This was his habit of assuming the martyr's role, while leaving himself an escape clause which enabled him to avoid making the supreme sacrifice. When *The Social Contract* was published in 1762, Rousseau insisted, against all advice, on signing the book, thereby making it certain not only that it would be banned but also that he would be arrested on charges which would lay him open to the death sentence. Before the warrant for his arrest was issued, he was, according to the custom of the day, forewarned so that he would have time to

escape and thereby relieve the authorities of the embarrassment
of having to carry out their sentence. He refused proudly:

They may take away my life, which has become a burden to me through
ill-health, but they cannot take away my freedom; Whatever they do, I
will still retain it, though I may be bound by their chains and confined
within their prison walls.

'It never occurred to him to take flight', says M. Guéhenno.
'Although his protectors were anxious for him to leave, his
calmness made them feel uneasy,' but within a few hours he had
in fact left. To have stayed would have compromised the Princesse de Luxembourg, one of the many aristocratic ladies whose
patronage he enjoyed.

   Later, when he had been allowed to return to Paris on
condition that he never published anything again, he decided
that he wanted his *Confessions* to be read in his lifetime and he
hit on the idea of entrusting the manuscript to God himself by
placing it on the high altar of Notre Dame, hoping that the stir
created by this act might bring it to the notice of the King.
However, when he entered Notre Dame, he found that the
chancel was enclosed by railings and that the gates were closed.
He had never noticed the railings before. As a result he was
prevented from taking provocative action and could continue to
live unmartyred.

   By this time Rousseau was mad. For the last sixteen years of
his life he undoubtedly suffered from persecution mania, a fact
which makes any appraisal of his personality extraordinarily
difficult. M. Guéhenno does not think in psychopathological
terms and he tends to interpret Rousseau's madness as the result
of his determination to be sincere at all costs – 'Jean-Jacques was
so sincere that he went mad' – and he sees him as an example of
La Rochefoucauld's maxim that 'Sincerity is a desire to compensate for one's defects and even to reduce their importance by
winning credit for admitting them.' He also attaches considerable importance to the fact that Rousseau had life-long stricture
of the urethra which made him dependent on a catheter and led
to recurrent attacks of uraemia.

   M. Guéhenno gives, however, such a detailed account of

Rousseau's life and habits and shows such an intimate understanding of his thought that he does, in fact, paint a clearer clinical picture of Rousseau's psychosis than he himself presumably realizes. Rousseau's illness indeed bears a striking resemblance to that of Schreber (whom I mention in 'Soul Murder' and 'Selfhood and Self-Awareness'), on whose autobiography Freud based his seminal study of the psychopathology of paranoia in 1911.

According to Freud, 'Schreber believed that he had a mission to redeem the world and to restore it to its lost state of bliss. This, however, he could only bring about if he were first transformed into a woman.' Rousseau not only believed that he had a mission to restore Man to his pristine state of being a noble savage, freed from his chains, but he also believed that he had become a woman. In the year from which Guéhenno dates his madness he abandoned trousers for a long Armenian robe which he decorated with silk sashes and fur trimmings, and in the same year he announced: 'I have thought like a man. I have written like a man, and people have disapproved of me, so now I will become a woman,' adding that 'he was savouring the pleasure of existence'. Freud interpreted the persecutory delusions of male paranoiacs as a defence and disguised expression of the repressed wish to be loved as a woman, and Rousseau's relationship with Hume is certainly open to this interpretation. Guéhenno describes two occasions on which Rousseau smothered Hume with kisses, but he later became convinced that Hume was the centre of a plot against him. And when they once shared a hotel bedroom, Rousseau was incensed to hear Hume exclaim several times during the night, 'Je tiens Jean-Jacques Rousseau.' Hume, commonsensical as ever, thought it unlikely that he spoke French in his sleep, and took the view that, in any case, he could hardly be held responsible for what he might have said then.

Guéhenno also leaves his readers in no doubt that Rousseau believed either that he was God or that at least he had special access to him, a conviction which runs parallel to Schreber's belief that he was God's Spouse.

Another curious detail of Rousseau's illness is that he thought he was being accused of trying to poison his friends, while at the same time he took to urging young women to feed their babies themselves. Perhaps he was struggling with a nagging suspicion that his ideas were not so beneficial to man after all.

1966

19

On Selfhood and Self-Awareness

As I mention in the Introduction, this essay is new and has not been published elsewhere. It was triggered off by rereading a review I had written for *Modern Painters* of a book on self-portraiture, but much of the thinking behind it must have been done some years ago, to judge by some undated notes on selfhood that I found among my papers.

One of the most puzzling problems which psychohistorians will eventually have to solve is the origin of the Judaeo-Christian tradition that it is only God who possesses full selfhood. No good Jew, I understand, will ever utter the word Jahweh, Jehovah, since it means I AM and only God can decently and truthfully say that. The underlying idea is, if I understand it rightly, that human beings are creatures, creations of God, and are therefore objects in his consciousness and not subjects of consciousness in their own right. It is He who is aware of them, and self-awarness, self-assertion, constitute acts of defiance of His will. It is He who has authority, who is the author of all things, and any human being who asserts himself, who claims to be an author, an authority, a creator, is claiming Godlike powers for himself, and will therefore incur the wrath of God.

One of the traditional interpretations of the Fall of Man implies the same idea. When Adam and Eve disobeyed God and ate of the Tree of Knowledge, it was self-knowledge, self-awareness (not sexual knowledge), that they acquired. From then onwards they not only did things but knew what they were doing when they did so, knew when they were naked and felt shame; and (as God Himself puts it in Genesis 3:22), 'the man is become as one of us, to know good and evil', and therefore liable to guilt.

The idea that it is dangerous for man to aspire to do and know things that only the Gods can do and know also appears in Greek mythology, where Prometheus's theft of the divine fire from Mount Olympus condemns him to eternal punishment. It seems that both the main cultures from which the Western tradition derives contain the idea that God, or the Gods, set limits on how self-aware and creative it is safe for a human being to aspire to be.

In Christianity itself, however, the concept of a Christ who is both God and Man makes it possible for man to participate in being God – since God is immanent as well as transcendental – and for mediation between Man and God to take place, so that an absolute confrontation between the self of man or woman and the selfhood of God can, in principle at least, be obviated. But I get the impression that the Churches have always looked askance at Christians whose awareness of God Immanent makes them forgetful of the authority of God Transcendental.

My reasons for starting this essay on self-awareness by talking about God will emerge as I proceed.

It is easy but, as I hope to show, misleading to assume that the self and the I, the ego, are identical and that consciousness of oneself is the same as the ability to say 'I want', 'I think'. Such a conflation is widespread, and one of the meanings of the word 'self' is undoubtedly simply to refer to, and to emphasize, that a person is asserting or affirming that it is he and not someone else who wants, thinks, imagines. 'I myself think' implies that there is someone else who does not so think. 'I myself told him' implies that someone else did not.

But there is another, more interesting, more peculiar usage which implies that the self and the 'I', the ego, are not only different from one another but can also be at odds with one another. 'I wanted to do such and such but would not have been true to myself if I had.' 'I wasn't myself when I did that.' 'I feel I haven't found myself yet.' All such phrases imply the existence of a self which is other than, and more than, any particular action I may make, which has some continuity, uniqueness and specificity which may N O T be reflected or expressed in any particular action I perform, or thought that I have, which continues to exist even if the contingencies of life or defensive manoeuvres prevent its expression.

In this sense, the self is that which one would be if contingencies or defences did not at times prevent one from being. 'With X I can be myself' implies that with some others one cannot. 'Until I left home (school, the army, etc.) I had no opportunity to be myself.' 'He (she) (my spouse, lover, psychotherapist, father-confessor) helped me to find myself.' The implication of all such statements is that everyone has a true self, that some people more or less lose it, that some of those who lose it more or less find it again, and that once found it is held on to more or less firmly. In this sense the self is that from which one can become alienated, from which, indeed, one is at all times at some risk of becoming alienated.

This self which is other than and in some sense more than the 'I' that asserts and affirms particular actions is assumed to possess certain attributes. One of these is continuity. This self that one is or has, is in or out of touch with, continues throughout life; despite growth, experience, and the accumulation of memories, the self remains the same self, in the same sense and to the same extent as a river remains the same river from its source to its mouth.

Another attribute of the self is consistency. Despite, again, growth and the accumulation of experience and memories, the self remains identifiably the same self throughout life. Some consistency of pattern remains.

Another is uniqueness. Each self is assumed to be in some essential way unlike all other selves, this unlikeness subsisting in the pattern, in the organization, and not merely in the fact that the contingencies of life ensure that every one has different experiences and memories.

Another attribute is that there is, it seems, an inherent moral necessity for the self to preserve its continuity, consistency and uniqueness; as a result of which it itself registers occasions on which the 'I' has breached its (the self's) continuity, has been untrue to its own consistency, has imitated or pretended to be someone else (some other self).

I should perhaps add that the moral – or should it be 'biological'? – necessity to be true to oneself is a matter of *internal* continuity, consistency and uniqueness, not of conformity to *external* criteria. It would, I conceive, be possible to emigrate, change one's name, one's profession, one's religion, one's political opinions and still be true to oneself; and to maintain the same position and opinions throughout life and be untrue to oneself. What is at stake is the maintenance of a consistent, continuous, unique pattern of growth in a changing world, and given the contingencies of history and life, internal and external consistency do not necessarily correspond.

At some point in childhood we become capable of introspection, of perceiving and observing ourselves and of comparing ourselves with others. When this happens, self-awareness dawns and we become capable of self-evaluation. The self in a sense becomes duplex, not only an experiencing subject but also its own object, and from then on we can take up moral and affective attitudes towards ourselves. As a result, self-awareness is accompanied by both momentary and more or less permanent emotional and moral attitudes towards oneself – self-love, self-hatred, self-contempt, complacency, self-criticism, self-indulgence, etc.

It is tempting, indeed, to say that it is possible for the self to feel about itself anything that it can feel about someone else, that it can love, hate, esteem itself, be suspicious of, contemptuous of, disappointed in, disparaging of, hard on, kind to, realistic or unrealistic about, puzzled by, etc., itself, just as it (we, one) may be all these things about someone else. And it is tempting too to assert that such characteristic or consistent attitudes of the self to itself bear a historical relationship to the attitudes that others took up towards the self when it was emerging, and that the person who is habitually self-critical, self-punitive, self-congratulatory, etc., is continuing and repeating the attitudes that were taken up towards him by those who reared and educated him.

This must, indeed, often be the case, and the fact that it is so is the reason why Freud, initially at least, located self-observation in the super-ego, which he regarded as the precipitate or internalization of the authority figures of childhood. But as he, and more particularly later analysts eventually realized, what is internalized is not necessarily a realistic picture of those authority figures as they actually regarded their child, but a distorted picture, the distortion being in the direction of either malignancy or benignness – so that, for instance, a child could impute a degree of cruelty and intolerance to its parents that they did not possess, and then incorporate cruelty and intolerance into its super-ego, thereby setting the stage for a later obsessional neurosis; or alternatively a child could impute a degree of complacent acceptance of itself that its parents did not in fact have, thereby setting the stage for later smugness.

In both cases, something complicated has happened; the development of self-awareness has been interfered with, intruded upon by defensive manoeuvres (projection, denial) which have compelled the obsessional to use his relationship with himself as the arena on which he enacts aggressive impulses, and the smug person to deny both that others may feel critical of him or that he needs on occasion to scrutinize himself critically. In each case we are encountering pathology.

There are, however, two types of feeling which the self can have about others which it is hard to conceive that it can have about itself. The first is envy. Self-satisfaction, self-contempt, self-doubt, self-pity, self-approbation, self-disparagement – these are all familiar states of mind which we cannot but have observed in ourselves or others. But self-envy? The phrase sounds odd, and it is hard to believe that anyone could begrudge his own good fortune. If people disparage themselves or their own good fortune we are, I think, more likely to assume that they feel guilty or are hoping to defuse the envy of others than that they are envious of themselves – this despite the fact that disparagement of other people's achievements or good fortune is commonly interpreted as envy, and, at a more sophisticated level of interpretation, admiration and idealization of others is not uncommonly interpreted as a defence against envy. But nonetheless there remains something strange about the idea that a tendency to disparage oneself might really indicate one's profound envy of oneself. The idea seems to involve a grossly divided self, such that a person fails to appreciate that aspects of himself which others regard as his good fortune are in fact parts of himself.

I can, however, imagine an artist envying his creative self and complaining that everyone pays attention to his art and never to himself in tones reminiscent of a child complaining that no one ever pays any attention to him now that his baby brother or sister has arrived, but I nonetheless find it hard to imagine such an artist actually formulating his complaint in terms of envy.

Rather similarly, people who inherit high social rank may resent the attention, respect and deference it wins them and feel that their 'real' human self gets neglected, but I doubt whether they would ever say that they envied their own social rank. Such people have in any case socially induced problems about their own selfhood and identity, since society confronts them with the task of assimilating their private discovery of self-awareness with the public imposition of a ready-made identity. 'I am I,' 'I am John Brown,' 'I am Lord Brown,' 'I am the King of X' all appear to be simple self-affirming statements indicating who one is, but in fact they differ in their frames of reference. The first is a statement that one has achieved differentiation from others. (The German philosopher Fichte the elder is reputed to have insisted upon celebrating not his children's birthdays, but the anniversaries of the day on which they first referred to themselves as 'I', this being the day on which they first became persons. One wonders what Frau Fichte thought about this.) 'I am John Brown' is a statement establishing one's social location by stating that one is one of the Brown family but not Thomas, Richard or Henry Brown, while the statements 'I am Lord Brown' and 'I am the King of X' are also assertions about how much and what kind of social power one wields, and what kind of deference one expects.

Although these possibilities of self-envy seem to arise solely from a logical and social confusion between selfhood as self-awareness and identity as social position within the social structure, this is not so, as two sets of phenomena show. The first is that people may describe and record changes in self-awareness by changing their names; in health, by insisting at a certain age that their childhood nicknames be abandoned in favour of their 'real' names (particularly obviously when that nickname was Baby or Babs); in illness, by giving themselves a new, and usually grand, name when a sense of self has been (pseudo-) recovered after a psychotic breakdown involving a loss of identity. For instance, Paul Schreber, the paranoid judge about whom Freud wrote a famous paper, and whom I have twice referred to in earlier essays in this volume, created himself Margrave of Tuscany and Tasmania when he ceased to feel himself a nonentity and again became Someone.

The second is that the nomenclature of social rank uses terms which derive from, and really only make sense when applied to, states of self-awareness. The words 'grace', 'serenity', 'nobility', have clear if difficult meanings when applied to people's personalities – they all refer to self-aware calm, imperturbable, generous, unenvious states of mind – but they are also used in Europe to designate rank. In Britain, Dukes, Duchesses and Archbishops are graces; abroad Highnesses can be serene; and the nobility are indiscriminately noble and honourable. The underlying assumption must be (have been) that it is possible to assimilate levels, stages, of self-awareness to levels, ranks, of the social order, though this assumption must have arisen more as a pious ideal wish than as a reality. Restless, anxious, clumsy, awkward, selfish, mean and envious aristocrats must have been with us from the beginning.

The second type of feeling which one self can have about another but can hardly have about itself is desire. I say 'desire' not 'love' advisedly, since it is generally, and presumably correctly, assumed that one can love oneself, and that self-love, if it does not exclude love for others, is a desirable, if not unavoidable state of affairs. The basic Christian injunction is to love one's neighbours as one does oneself, and it has become a platitude among psychoanalysts that it is impossible to love others if one does not love oneself.

However, the fact that one can love oneself, and the likelihood that what used to be called the self-preservative instincts ensure that one cannot not love oneself, does not imply that one can desire oneself – if only because one can only desire what one has not got and desire must therefore always be directed towards what is other than oneself. The apparent exceptions to this are the sexual perversion of narcissism and that wider range of phenomena that are loosely and usually disparagingly referred to as narcissistic. But in true narcissism the object seems not to be the self pure and simple but the image and reflection of the self's body regarded as though it were an other. In the Greek myth Narcissus does not know that the image he desires is his own reflection, and it is his loneliness, the absence of any other, which determines that he falls in love with his own image and not with someone else. And contemporary analysts seem agreed that 'narcissistic' people are not, as Freud thought, those who have never grown out of some infantile stage of primary narcissism, but those who have failed to find an object, a reciprocating other, when they most needed one – and who have, therefore, had to exploit the fact that it is possible to use oneself, and images of oneself, as substitutes for others, by admiring oneself in mirrors, by talking to oneself, praising oneself, by touching and stimulating oneself while imagining someone else doing so.

To speak clinically for a moment, the use of oneself as a substitute for others, whether as a source of love or of developmental or erotic stimulation, seems to be a hazardous move, since it may initiate a line of development which eventually precludes interaction with others. What may have started as an absence of others, or rejection by others, or non-comprehension by others, may turn into avoidance of others, rejection of others, suspicion of all others. Hence the aloof independence of those who cannot accept help from others, the opinionatedness of auto-didacts, the inaccessibility, real or apparent, complete or partial, to psychotherapy of 'narcissistic characters', and (perhaps) of schizophrenics and autistic children. What seems to have happened to such people is that their capacity for interaction with others has got caught up in a world of mirror images of themselves. As a result the significant events in their lives are not the various relationships they have had with other people but shifts in their relationship with themselves, and anyone who, like a lover or a therapist, seeks to establish a relationship with them, finds him- or herself caught up not with the ghosts of past real others but with reflections of past and present selves.

In addition to the various feelings that anyone may have towards himself which parallel feelings he may have towards others, there are also a number of emotions which can only be felt about oneself, which are contingent on the development of self-awareness, and which one cannot conceive an infant or an animal having. These emotions may be either pleasant or unpleasant, the pleasant ones being feelings of achievement and self-fulfilment, self-respect and, in some senses of a most difficult word, pride; the unpleasant ones being guilt and shame. (For the moment I am deliberately ignoring the complications produced by the fact that one can experience these emotions, both the pleasant and the unpleasant ones, directly in respect of people with whom one identifies and imaginatively in respect of people with whom one can empathize.)

My interest here is with the unpleasant emotions, guilt and shame. Guilt can only occur in someone who can formulate thoughts such as 'I have done wrong' or 'I have been naughty', thoughts which require self-awareness in the way that 'X is angry with me for having done something he doesn't like' or 'Mummy is cross with me' do not, since, first, their emphasis is on the fact that I have done something not on the fact that someone else is reacting to an action of mine, and, secondly, the person thinking the thought and feeling guilty himself endorses the idea that he has infringed some regulation that he himself considers binding. In other words a person feeling guilty must possess some awareness of himself as a free agent who could have refrained from performing the guilt-inducing act, and an awareness that the society or group or family to which he belongs has certain rules that are binding.

Furthermore, anyone feeling guilt can, I think, formulate in some terms or other why these rules are binding, even though his formulations may not amount to more than 'Mummy and

Daddy say so' or because God or the Church or the Party forbids it. The further question as to why Mummy and Daddy say so or why the Church or the Party forbids it can only be raised by people whose self-awareness has reached a further level of sophistication at which it becomes possible to question the validity of the regulations imposed by authority. Typically, this higher level of self-awareness is only reached, if it ever is, in adolescence. Presumably it can only be risked after one has ceased to be totally dependent on one's immediate authorities and can at least envisage the possibility of surviving without their protection. Presumably, too, the discovery that authorities do not always agree with one another, that parents, priests and teachers do not always see eye to eye, and that other countries, other cultures, have different values, must also facilitate the capacity to question the assumptions made by one's own background and the desire to work out one's own code for deciding what actions should arouse guilt.

It will be noted that I have been assuming the existence of two levels of self-awareness, one appropriate to childhood and life within a small and morally homogeneous group, and another appropriate to the wider and morally heterogeneous world of adult life. At the first level, the child is aware of itself as a relatively free agent within a small group whose rules it is aware of and regards as part of the natural order of things, being as yet too helpless to afford to question them. At the second level, the adolescent or adult is aware of him- or herself as a potentially much freer agent living within a larger group whose rules he or she has to discover and which he or she may or may not endorse. I have also been assuming that this second level of self-awareness is not achieved or even attempted by everyone, even in complex, literate societies such as our own, in which the evidence for the relativity of values and the data necessary for starting to question all received notions are not all that inaccessible.

The reasons for this failure to achieve the second level of self-awareness are multitudinous, but can, I think, be divided into two groups, those based on loyalty and those based on the fear of committing hubris. Loyalty tends to make one feel that one is betraying one's group of origin if one questions its values; it is

responsible for the conservative inertia present in both individuals and societies. The fear of hubris, the fear that to think,
to act, truly for oneself, from the ground of one's own being and
nobody else's, would be to oppose some omnipotent power who
alone can be Himself or Herself, to bring the wrath of God down
upon one, or to risk being pursued by the Furies. It is the
constant fear that to be fully one's own person, to be totally self-
aware, is arrogant, insolent and dangerous, that puts limits on
the achievement of self-awareness. It is also the reason why I
started this essay by drawing attention to the presence in the
Western tradition of the idea that it is wicked and dangerous to
claim to be a creator not a creature and to be oneself not the
creation of some other self.

The self-awareness of poets, writers, painters and others who
do claim to be creative is complicated by the fact that this claim
lays them open to the charge of arrogance. In former times they
defended themselves against this charge by invoking the concept
of inspiration. Their creative activity was not an act of self-
assertion, self-expression or self-fulfilment but one of passivity
towards the muse who inspired them, or alternatively they were
merely the vessel, the mouthpiece, through which God, or some
other Other, spoke. H. Rider Haggard in his private diaries gave
a revealing and amusing example of how Kipling reconciled his
creativity with the modesty becoming to a gentleman:

He [Kipling] went on to show that anything which any of us did *well*
was no credit to us; that it came from somewhere else: 'We are only
telephone wires.' As an example he instanced (I think) *Recessional* in his
own case, and *She* in mine. 'You didn't write *She*, you know,' he said.
'Someone wrote it through you!' Or some such words.

Modern post-Freudian artists and writers have, however, no
choice but to admit that it is indeed they themselves who write
their books or paint their pictures; and they only lay themselves
open to the charge of arrogance if they claim to do so totally
unaided and to have acquired nothing from their parents, their
teachers and their predecessors. (I discussed the psychology of
such people in 'On Ablation of the Parental Images, or The
Illusion of Having Created Oneself' in *Psychoanalysis and*

Beyond.) The idea that creative activity is in some sense passive seems, however, to be psychologically sound. The 'I', the ego, the Persona, of the creative person has to be able to be passive and receptive towards his wider self, be able to allow himself 'negative capability' in his attitude towards his wider self and its (his) imagination. (I consider this matter more fully earlier on in this collection in 'Remembering, Imagining, Creating', and also in Chapters 3 and 9 of *The Innocence of Dreams.*)

The self-awareness of modern man, and in particular of creative people, must have been modified and possibly increased by advances in technology. It must be one thing to reread a book one has oneself written in manuscript and another to read it in print. The latter has acquired an objectivity and impersonality the other lacks, which must, I conceive, modify the feedback an author gets from rereading his own books. Mirrors, which were first manufactured on a commercial scale in the early sixteenth century (not long after the invention of printing) and only became cheap in the late seventeenth century, must have made it much easier literally to see oneself as others see us, and their availability must be what made self-portraiture a recognized genre of painting.

In *Sincerity and Authenticity*, Lionel Trilling points out that, according to many social historians, 'something like a mutation in human nature' occurred in the late sixteenth and early seventeenth centuries, as a result of which people became more aware of themselves as individual selves unlike other selves, and more inclined to assume that their private subjective experiences were worth exploring and could and should be of interest to others. Lacan and others have suggested that this increased awareness and interest in Self was due to the availability of mirrors, so it seems likely that our contemporary self-awareness is influenced, modified and perhaps increased by our familiarity with external images of our bodily self derived from mirrors, photographs and home movies. Such images cannot be a matter of indifference since we are bound at times to wonder how much they reveal of our inner, subjective self and how accurately or inaccurately they correspond to it. We also have access, in a way that earlier generations did not, to records of how numerous others have experienced themselves in their self-portraits, their autobiographies, their novels. The *Shorter Oxford English Dictionary* gives support to the idea that the self is a fairly recent preoccupation, naming 1674 as the earliest date for the use of the word to mean 'that which in a person is really and intrinsically *he*' and 'a permanent subject of successive and varying states of consciousness'.

In view of the fact that the popularization of Freudian ideas has made everyone aware of the existence of a neurotic sense of guilt, of the fact that one can feel guilt that one does *not* endorse as justified, it is perhaps necessary to affirm that the capacity to feel guilty is not necessarily neurotic, and that awareness of oneself as a member of a group cannot but create the potentiality of feeling guilty, since it cannot but happen that one will at times want to do things that would injure another member of that group, that one will at times want to do things that would injure someone one loves. (Presumably a self-aware person always knows whom he loves.) One would get more attention if one's sibling died or if one killed him, one would get one parent to oneself if the other vanished – these are guilt-inducing thoughts that are bound in the nature of things to arise. It would only be in a world with a superabundance of both love and commodities that covetousness, envy and jealousy would never be provoked. Guilt must indeed be a necessary emotion, assisting self-aware people to live within groups by restraining them from acting on wishes that run counter to the needs of other members – or, to be pedantic, it is the awareness of the possibility of feeling guilt that is the restraint, while the actual feeling it is the inner sanction, imposed by one's awareness of the awareness of others.

Many if not most of the actions that occasion guilt are specifiable and codifiable. If one feels guilty, one can usually specify precisely which of one's past actions is making one feel this and give a name to the offence that one has committed. If I take something knowing that it is someone else's, I know that I have committed theft. If I were to kill someone, I would know that I had committed murder. If I say something I know is untrue, I know I have told a lie. In all such cases, both the action inducing the feeling of guilt and the nature of the offence are known and specifiable. As a result of this, and of the not unconnected fact that guilt-inducing acts are social actions, acts of either commission or omission, guilt-provoking actions can be codified into legal systems. And, as a further result, uncertainties may arise as to whether one feels guilty because one has done something that one oneself feels to be wrong or whether one has infringed a legal or moral system that one in general endorses. Discrepancies may therefore arise between the subjective feeling of guilt and the objective (if that's the right word) fact of being guilty in law. It is possible to continue to feel guilty after being acquitted on a technicality, and not to feel guilty after being convicted of a crime that lies outside one's own moral code.

Moral codes can include *intentions* among the acts about which one should feel guilty, which is something that legal systems cannot consider apart from an action, except in particular instances, such as conspiracy. The Ten Commandments certainly assert that one is, and should feel, guilty if one kills, steals, bears false witness, commits adultery or bows down before a graven image. All of these are straightforwardly actions which one either has or has not performed. But the commandments also affirm that one is, and should feel, guilty if one coverts one's neighbour's wife or his ox or his ass 'or anything that is his', or fails to honour one's parents, despite the fact that coveting and failing to honour are not actions but thoughts, passing or recurring intentions, which may never be acted upon. The idea that one should feel guilty about even momentarily thinking of injuring another is the reverse of closing the stable door after the horse has fled and is, mercifully, one which, for practical reasons, legal systems rarely have to take account of. It implies, and encourages, the development of a peculiar distortion of self-awareness, in which moral self-scrutiny becomes the major function of consciousness. The ideal ceases to be self-knowledge, self-acceptance, self-fulfilment. Instead it is seen as the achievement of moral perfection and the elimination of all those human impulses incompatible with such perfection, thus transforming self-awareness from awareness of oneself in relation to the awareness of others, into awareness of oneself in relation to the imagined source or author of the ideal of perfection: often to a notion of God.

My reason for emphasizing that guilt is typically felt in relation to acts that are codifiable and specifiable is that it differs strikingly in this respect from shame, which may be felt under conditions in which one is at a loss to say precisely what it is that is making one feel ashamed. Shame presupposes the existence of some ideal conception of oneself – psychoanalysis calls it the ego-ideal – and the emotion occurs if one senses or imagines that one is failing to live up to that ideal, that one is, as one says, letting oneself down. Some of the most obvious examples of shame occur in childhood, when children who are proud of the fact that they no longer cry, wet or soil themselves, discover to their embarrassment that they are not immune to such mishaps. Similarly, adults feel ashamed, are crestfallen, if they are exposed as incompetent and ignorant in any field in which they take pride. Men are ashamed, not guilty, if they are impotent.

Shame is indeed the reverse of pride, and just as a person can take proper pride in his appearance, his health, his achievements, his experience, or can display false pride (hauteur) based on pretentiousness and illusions about himself, so a person can feel proper shame – it is an insult to call someone shameless – about failures to live up to his own standards and false shame if his pretensions and illusions are exploded. As Helen Merrell Lynd, in particular, long ago pointed out (in *On Shame and the Search for Identity*, 1958), private experiences of shame are perceptions of aspects of oneself that one has not included in one's conception of oneself; they reveal, therefore, that one's self-concept is either incomplete or distorted. Public experiences of shame, however, are perceptions that one's idea of one's relationship to the outside world, to others, has been incorrect or inadequate. In both cases the emotion can be a stimulus which makes people more realistic about their own nature and place in the world, and which helps them to recover self-respect in the process. I imagine that most people's most acute experiences of shame are in adolescence, when their bodily and mental selves and their positions in the world are changing rapidly.

It would seem, then, that as we acquire self-awareness we also become susceptible to the fear of being punished for committing hubris; and will at times inevitably feel the emotions of guilt and shame, experiences which may either increase self-knowledge and enhance self-awareness or invoke defences, such as splitting, denial and projection, which distort and limit self-awareness and increase alienation. This is the price we pay for eating of the Tree of Knowledge.

1990

Sigmund Freud, 'Psychoanalytic Notes on an Autobiographical Account of a Case of Paranoia (Dementia Paranoides)', SE, vol. 12 (London: The Hogarth Press, 1958).

Erich Fromm, You Shall Be As Gods (New York: Holt, Rinehart & Winston, 1967).

R. D. Laing, The Divided Self (London: Tavistock, 1960).

The Self and Others (London: Tavistock, 1961).

Helen Merrell Lynd, On Shame and the Search for Identity (London: Routledge & Kegan Paul, 1958).

William McDougall, An Introduction to Social Psychology, 22nd edition (London: Merton, 1988).

G. Piers and M. Singer, Shame and Guilt (Springfield, Ill.: Charles C. Thomas, 1953).

Charles Rycroft, The Innocence of Dreams (London: The Hogarth Press, 1979, 1991).

Psychoanalysis and Beyond (London: The Hogarth Press, 1985).

W. Scott and M. Clifford, 'Self Envy and Envy of Dreams and Dreaming', International Review of Psychoanalysis, vol. 2, part 3 (1975).

Lionel Trilling, Sincerity and Authenticity (London: Oxford University Press, 1972).

Complete Bibliography

Essays marked with an asterisk are included in the present volume.

1951
'A Contribution to the Study of the Dream Screen'. *Int. J. Psycho-Anal.*, vol. 32, and *Imagination and Reality*, pp. 1–13.

1953
'Some Observations on a Case of Vertigo'. *Int. J. Psycho-Anal.*, vol. 34, and *Imagination and Reality*, pp. 14–28.

1956
'Symbolism and Its Relationship to the Primary and Secondary Processes'. *Int. J. Psycho-Anal.*, vol. 37, and *Imagination and Reality*, pp. 42–60.

1957
Review of *Peter and Caroline: A Child Asks about Childbirth and Sex* by Sten Hegeler. *Int. J. Psycho-Anal.*, vol. 38.

1958
'An Enquiry into the Function of Words in the Psycho-analytical Situation'. *Int. J. Psycho-Anal.*, vol. 39, and *Imagination and Reality*, pp. 69–83.
Review of *On Shame and the Search for Identity* by Helen Merrell Lynd. *Int. J. Psycho-Anal.*, vol. 39.
Review of *Neurotic Distortion of the Creative Process* by Lawrence S. Kubie. *Int. J. Psycho-Anal.*, vol. 39.

1959
Review of *The Quest for Identity* by Allen Wheelis. *Int. J. Psycho-Anal.*, vol. 40.
'The Luther Case'. Review of *Young Man Luther* by Erik Erikson. *Observer*, 13 December.
'The Disciples of Freud'. Review of *Freud and the Post-Freudians* by J. A. C. Brown. *Observer*.
Review of *The Integrity of the Personality* by Anthony Storr. *Observer*, 10 July.

1960
'The Analysis of a Paranoid Personality'. *Int. J. Psycho-Anal.*, vol. 41, and *Psychoanalysis and Beyond*, pp. 233–58.

'Scream from the Grave'. Review of *Fear, Punishment, Anxiety and the Wolfenden Report* by Charles Berg. *Observer*, 3 January.
'Married Couples in Conflict'. Review of *Marriage: Studies in Emotional Conflict and Growth*, ed. Lily Pincus. *Observer*, 28 January.

1961
Review of *Personality Structure and Human Interaction* by Harry Guntrip. *Int. J. Psycho-Anal.*, vol. 42, and *Psychoanalysis and Beyond*, pp. 132–9.
'Problem Children'. Review of *Delinquent and Neurotic Children* by Ivy Bennett. *Observer*, 5 February.
'In Our Time: The Kleinian Viewpoint'. *Observer*, 9 April, and *Psychoanalysis and Beyond*, pp. 128–31.
'Freud as a Father Figure'. Review of *Letters of Sigmund Freud 1873–1939*, ed. Ernst L. Freud. *Observer*, 18 June.

1962
'On the Defensive Function of Schizophrenic Thinking and Delusion-Formation'. *Int. J. Psycho-Anal.*, vol. 43, and *Imagination and Reality*, pp. 84–101.
'Beyond the Reality Principle'. *Int. J. Psycho-Anal.*, vol. 43, and *Imagination and Reality*, pp. 102–13.
'Discipline for Young Children – at Home. By a practising psychoanalyst'. *Where*, Summer.
'Leonardo Psychoanalysed'. Review of *Leonardo da Vinci* by K. R. Eissler. *Observer*, 8 April.
'Naivety of Melanie Klein'. Review of *Our Adult World and Other Essays* by Melanie Klein. *Observer*.
'Priest, Philosopher and Physician'. Review of *Three Hundred Years of Psychiatry 1535–1860*, by Richard Hunter and Ida Macalpine. *Observer*.

1963
'Corrupted by a Mystique?' Review of *The Feminine Mystique* by Betty Friedan. *New Society*, 6 June.
'Psychiatric Orthodoxy Contradicted'. Review of *A Study of Brief Psychotherapy* by Dr D. H. Malan. *New Society*, 3 October.
'Freud and the Romans'. Review of *Problems in Psychoanalysis: A Symposium*, ed. C. Batten. *New Society*, 17 October.
'Freud and the Pastor'. Review of *Psycho-Analysis and Faith: The Letters of Sigmund Freud and Oskar Pfister*, ed. Heinrich Meng and Ernst Freud. *Observer*, 15 December.

1964
'Analysing Freud'. Review of *Freud* by Reuben Fine. *Observer*, 16 February.
'Post Freudian'. Review of *Introduction to the Work of Melanie Klein* by Hanna Segal. *Observer*, 5 April.
'Beyond the Panel'. Review of *Fringe Medicine* by Brian Inglis. *New Society*, 30 April.
'To Touch Us'. Review of 'Art as Communication', an exhibition of art by psychiatric patients at the ICA. *New Society*, 14 May.
'"Improvements" in Psychiatry'. Review of *Psychotherapy: Purchase of Friendship* by W. Schofield. *New Society*, 20 August.

'The Care of the Insane'. Review of *The Indications of Insanity* by John Conolly. *Observer*, 23 August.

'The Emergence of Psychology'. Review of *A Hundred Years of Psychology* by J. C. Flugel and *A Short History of British Psychology* by L. S. Hearnshaw. *New Society*, 17 September.

'Therapist and Patient'. Review of *An Introduction to Psychotherapy* by Sidney Tarachow. *New Society*, 26 November.

* 'Look Back in Loathing'. Review of *Words* by Jean-Paul Sartre. *New Society*, 3 December.

1965

'The Effect of the Psychoneurotic Patient on his Environment'. *The Role of Psychosomatic Disorder in Adult Life*, ed. J. Wisdom and H. Wolff. Oxford: Pergamon Press, 1965. See also *Imagination and Reality*, pp. 129–35.

'Being Changed by Language'. Review of *Linguistic Change in Present-day English* by Charles Barber. *New Society*, 21 January.

'Two Sides of Eysenck'. Review of *Fact and Fiction in Psychology* by H. J. Eysenck. *Observer*, 21 March.

'A Conspiracy of Victims'. Review of *Pedophilia and Exhibitionism* by J. W. Mohr, R. E. Turner and M. B. Jerry. *New Society*.

'The It and the Id'. Review of *The Wild Analyst* by Carl and Sylvia Grossman. *Observer*, 13 June.

'Friend of Freud'. Review of *The Freud Journal of Lou Andreas-Salome* by Stanley A. Leavy. *Observer*, 15 August.

Review of *Contemporary Schools of Psychology* by Robert S. Woodworth in collaboration with Mary R. Sheeham. *New Society*, 25 September.

'Even Patients are Human'. Review of *Introduction to Psychology for Medical Students* by R. R. Hetherington, D. H. Miller and J. G. Neville. *New Society*, 16 October.

'Guide to Freud'. Review of *What Freud Really Said* by David Stafford-Clark. *Observer*, 21 November.

'A Disease of People'. Review of *Hysteria: the History of a Disease* by Ilza Veith. *New Society*, 23 November.

'On Ablation of the Parental Images'. Unpublished article, rev. 1973. First published in *Psychoanalysis and Beyond*, pp. 214–32.

1966

'Causes and Meaning'. *Psychoanalysis Observed*, ed. Charles Rycroft. London: Constable, 1966, and Harmondsworth: Penguin Books, 1968, pp. 7–22. See also *Psychoanalysis and Beyond*, pp. 41–51.

'Cheering Up Freud'. Review of *A Psychoanalytic Dialogue: The Letters of Sigmund Freud and Karl Abraham 1907–1926*, ed. Hilda C. Abraham and Ernst Freud. *Observer*, 21 January.

'Should Inauthenticity be Punished?' Review of *One in Twenty* by Brian Magee. *New Society*, 2 April.

'A Foray against Ghosts'. Review of *Eliminating the Unconscious: A Behaviourist View of Psychoanalysis* by T. R. Miles. *New Society*, 30 June.

'Striptease with the Clothes On'. Review of *If Hopes were Dupes* by Catherine York. *New Society*, 7 July.

'In Abstract-Cuckooland'. Review of *The Triumph of the Therapeutic* by Philip Rieff. *New Society*, 11 August.

'Sleeping Like a Baby'. Review of *Medical and Dental Hypnosis and its Clinical Applications* by J. Hartland. *New Society*, 11 August.

* 'Man and Superwoman'. Review of *Jean-Jacques Rousseau* by J. M. Guéhenno. *New Society*, 1 September.

'Light on Jung'. Review of *What Jung Really Said* by E. A. Bennet. *Observer*, 11 September.

'The Origins of Fighting'. Review of *On Aggression* by Konrad Lorenz. *New Society*, 15 September.

'Ashes, Old Boy – Just Ashes'. Review of *The Life of Ian Fleming* by John Pearson. *New Society*, 1 December.

'Grassroots Oddities'. Review of *The Social Psychology of Social Movements* by Hans Toch. *New Society*, 22 December.

1967

'The God I Want'. *The God I Want*, ed. James Mitchell. London: Constable, pp. 25–41. See also *Psychoanalysis and Beyond*, pp. 281–94.

'Knees under the Table'. Review of *ESP: A Scientific Evaluation* by C. E. M. Hansel. *New Society*, 9 March.

'Patients in Prison'. Review of *Psychopathic Disorders and Their Assessment* by M. Craft. *New Society*, 26 January.

'Muddle in Massachusetts'. Review of *The Boston Strangler* by Gerold Frank. *New Society*, 16 February.

'The Games Society Chooses'. Review of *Being Mentally Ill* by Thomas J. Scheff. *New Society*, 20 April.

* 'Lost Children'. Review of *The Empty Fortress* by Bruno Bettelheim. *New York Review of Books*, 4 May. (Published in this volume as part of 'Soul Murder and Survival'.)

'Priest and Psychotherapist'. Review of *A Fortunate Man* by John Berger. *New Society*, 11 May.

'The Necessity of Anxiety'. Review of *Psychology and the Human Dilemma* by Rollo May. *New Society*, 27 July.

'Awful Warnings'. Review of *The Anxiety-Makers* by Alex Comfort. *Observer*, 30 July.

'Avoiding the Stigmata'. Review of *The Clock of Competence* by Robert B. Edgerton. *New Society*, 17 August.

'Of Mice and Men'. Review of *The American Male* by Myron Brenton. *New Society*, 7 September.

'The Growth of Humanism'. Review of *You Shall be as Gods* by Eric Fromm. *New Society*, 14 September.

'Holons and Hierarchies'. Review of *The Ghost in the Machine* by Arthur Koestler. *New Society*, 19 October.

'Biography: Brotherly Hatred'. Review of *Friendship and Fratricide* by Meyer A. Zeligs. *TLS*, 9 November.

'Uninhibited'. Review of *The Use of Lateral Thinking* by Edward de Bono. *TLS*, 30 November.

Review of *Two Wise Children* by Robert Graves and *Gertrude's Child* by Richard Hughes. *New Society*, 7 December.

'Prospectors of the Unconscious'. Review of *Freud and his Early Circle* by Vincent Brome. *Observer*, 24 December.

1968

Imagination and Reality: Psycho-Analytical Essays 1951–1961. Intro. M. Masud R. Khan and Joan D. Sutherland. London: The Hogarth Press and The Institute of Psycho-Analysis.

A Critical Dictionary of Psychoanalysis. London: Nelson; reprinted in paperback, Harmondsworth: Penguin Books, 1972.

Anxiety and Neurosis. London: Allen Lane.

'Doctor's Psychotherapy'. Review of *Sexual Discord in Marriage* by Michael Courtenay. *New Society*, 28 March.

'Grande Dame'. Review of *Selected Problems of Adolescence* by Helene Deutsch. *New Society*, 23 May.

'Non-accidental Injuries'. Review of *The Battered Child* by Ray E. Helfer and Henry Kempe. *New Society*, 20 June.

'Drugs for the Mind'. Review of *Psychopharmacology*, ed. C. R. B. Joyce. *TLS*.

'Ouch!' Review of *Disease, Pain and Sacrifice* by David Bakan and *Individuality in Pain and Suffering* by Asenath Petrie. *NYRB*, 11 July.

'The Victims'. Review of *Death in Life: The Survivors of Hiroshima* by Robert Jay Lifton. *New Statesman*, 30 August.

'Why War?' Review of *Sanity and Survival: Psychological Aspects of War and Peace* by Jerome D. Frank. *New Society*, 3 October.

'The Suicidal Society'. Review of *Negations* by Herbert Marcuse. *New Statesman*.

'Under Stress'. Review of *Violence, Monkeys and Man* by Claire Russell and W. M. S. Russell. *New Statesman*, 8 November.

1969

'All in the Mind'. Review of *Analytical Psychology: Its Theory and Practice* by C. G. Jung. *NYRB*, 16 January, and *Psychoanalysis and Beyond*, pp. 113–16.

'Marriage Lines'. Review of *Marriage and Personal Development* by Rubin Blanck and Gertrude Blanck. *New Society*, 23 January.

'Mnemonists Never Forget'. Review of *The Mind of a Mnemonist* by A. R. Luria. *TLS*, 20 February.

'On Tape'. Review of *The Twisting Lane* by Tony Parker. *New Society*, 20 February.

'Life Without Father'. Review of *Society Without the Father* by Alexander Mitscherlich. *Observer*, 9 March.

'Yes with Everything'. Review of *Individual Morality* by James Hemming. *New Society*, 27 March.

'What's So Funny?' Review of *Rationale of the Dirty Joke: An Analysis of Sexual Humor* by G. Legman. *NYRB*, 10 April.

* 'Model and Metaphor in Psychology'. Talk given in a discussion of this topic held in London on 7 May, organized by the Canadian Broadcasting Corporation.

'Psychology and Science: Playing at being Us'. Review of *The Presentation of Self in Everyday Life* by Erving Goffman. *TLS*, 8 May.

'Painful Subject'. Review of *The Spectrum of Pain* by Richard Serjeant. *New Society*, 15 May.

'Out of the Way: Memoirs of an Old Bolshevik'. *New Society*, 29 May, and *Psychoanalysis and Beyond*, pp. 207–13.

'Unattainable Aims of Psychoanalysis'. *TES*, 13 June.

'Analysing the Analyst'. *TES*, 20 June.
'A New Religion?' *TES*, 27 June.
'Psychoanalytical Insight'. *TES*, 4 July.
'The Origin of Love'. Review of *Attachment and Loss*, vol. I: *Attachment* by John Bowlby. *TLS*, 14 August. See also *Psychoanalysis and Beyond*, pp. 147–55.
'Freudian Slip'. Review of *Eros and Civilisation: A Philosophical Inquiry into Freud* by Herbert Marcuse. *New Society*, 25 September.
'The Royal Affliction'. Review of *George III and the Mad-Business* by Ida Macalpine and Richard Hunter. *Observer*, 16 November.
'The Case of Wilhelm Reich'. *NYRB*, 4 December.
* 'Why Psychiatry is an Intrinsically Odd Profession'. (Undated, 1960s.) Unpublished lecture (published for the first time in this volume).

1970
Anxiety and Neurosis. Harmondsworth: Penguin Books.
'Airy Thinking'. Review of *The Mechanism of Mind* by Edward de Bono. *TLS*, 12 February.
'Freudian Triangles'. Review of *Brother Animal: The Story of Freud and Tausk* by Paul Roazen. *Observer*, 26 April.
Review of *Human Sexual Inadequacy* by William H. Masters and Virginia E. Johnson. *Nature*, 25 July.

1971
Reich. London: Fontana.
'Among the Flower Children'. Review of *The Human Be-In* by Helen Perry. *New Statesman*, 1 January.
'The Psychology of Orgasm'. *Man and Woman*, 14 April, and *Psychoanalysis and Beyond*, pp. 167–75.
'Noes, Noses, Nonsense'. Review of *The Death of the Family* by David Cooper. *Guardian*, 25 May.
'Not So Much a Treatment, More a Way of Life'. Review of *The Wolf-Man by the Wolf-Man*, ed. Muriel Gardiner. *NYRB*, 21 October, and *Psychoanalysis and Beyond*, pp. 92–100.
'A Feeling in the Air'. Review of *Intimate Behaviour* by Desmond Morris. *New Statesman*, 15 October, and *Psychoanalysis and Beyond*, pp. 184–8.
'Ritual Joy'. Review of *Encounter Groups* by Carl R. Rogers and *Joy* by William C. Schutz. *New Society*, 11 November.
'Sampling Sex'. Review of *Sex and Marriage in England Today* by Geoffrey Gorer. *New Statesman*, 26 November.
'Madhouses'. Review of *The Trade in Lunacy* by William L. L. Parry-Jones, *New Statesman*.

1972
'Why Psychiatry is an Intrinsically Odd Profession'. Unpublished lecture first given at Bristol University Medical School, 25 January.
'Roots of Love'. Review of *Love and Hate* by Irenaus Eibi-Eibesfeldt. *New Society*, 10 February.
'Closed System'. Review of *Beyond Freedom and Dignity* by B. F. Skinner. *New Statesman*, 17 March.

'Unthinkable'. Review of *The Roots of Coincidence* by Arthur Koestler. *New Statesman*, 11 February.

'A Great Mother's Helper'. Review of *Playing and Reality* and *Therapeutic Consultations in Child Psychiatry* by D. W. Winnicott. *NYRB*, 1 June, and *Psychoanalysis and Beyond*, pp. 140–6.

'Still Outside'. Review of *New Pathways in Psychology* by Colin Wilson. *Spectator*, 27 May.

'You Never Can Tell'. Review of *Psychological Probability* by John Cohen. *New Statesman*, 23 June.

'Doctoring Freud'. Review of *Freud: Living and Dying* by Max Schur. *NYRB*, 10 August, and *Psychoanalysis and Beyond*, pp. 105–12.

'The Artist as Patient'. *TLS*, 22 September.

'Hybrid Monster'. Review of *Pornography: The Longford Report. TES*, 29 September.

'Stages of the Transference'. Review of *Freud* by Jonathan Miller. *Spectator*, 7 October.

'The Anatomy of Violence'. Unpublished lecture first delivered at the Social Responsibility Conference organized by The Bishop's Council for Social Responsibility, Coventry Cathedral, 4 December.

1973

* 'Agents and Patients'. Review of *Ideology and Insanity* by Thomas S. Szasz. *New Statesman*, 23 February. (Published in this volume as 'Szasz and the Myth of Mental Illness'.)

'Theory Games'. Review of *Encounters* by Erving Goffman. *TLS*, 1 March.

'Psychology: Tragic Romances'. Review of *Incest* by Herbert Maisch. *TES*, 2 March.

'Bions and Phantasies'. Review of *Wilhelm Reich: The Evolution of His Work* by David Boadella. *TES*, 30 March.

'Life with Father'. Review of *Soul Murder* by Morton Schatzman. *New Statesman*, 30 March, and *Psychoanalysis and Beyond*, pp. 101–4.

'Dead or Injured'. Review of *Violence in Human Society* by John Gunn. *New Society*, 21 June.

'Psychology: Experience, Not Fantasies'. Review of *Attachment and Loss*, vol. 2: *Separation: Anxiety and Anger*, by John Bowlby. *TES*, 29 June. See also *Psychoanalysis and Beyond*, pp. 147–55.

'Dog Beneath the Skin?' Review of *The Mind Possessed* by William Sargant. *Observer*, 14 October.

1974

'Is Freudian Symbolism a Myth?' *NYRB*, 24 January. See also *Symbols and Sentiments*, ed. Ioan Lewis. London: Academic Press, 1977, and *Psychoanalysis and Beyond*, pp. 64–78.

'Folie à Deux'. Review of *The Freud/Jung Letters: The Correspondence between Sigmund Freud and C. G. Jung*, ed. William McGuire. *NYRB*, 18 April.

* 'A Suitable Place for Treatment'. Review of *A Home for the Heart* by Bruno Bettelheim. *Observer*, 12 May. (Published in this volume as part of 'Soul Murder and Survival'.)

'Unhealthy Activities'. Review of *Creative Malady* by George Pickering. *Observer*, 6 October.

1975
'Freud and the Imagination'. *NYRB*, 3 April, and *Psychoanalysis and Beyond*, pp. 261–77.
'A Family and Its Head'. Review of *The Manson Murders* by Vincent Bugliosi. *TLS*, 18 April.
'Ideas of Madness'. Review of *Madness and Morals* by Vieda Skultans. *Observer*, 18 May.
* 'As the Apple to Its Core'. Review of *Transactional Analysis in Psychotherapy* by Eric Berne. *New Society*, 3 July. (Published in this volume as 'Berne and Games People Play'.)
'Miscalculated Risks'. Review of *The St Albans Poisoner* by Anthony Holden. *TLS*, 26 September.
'People before Rats'. Review of *Human Beings* by Liam Hudson. *TES*, 21 November.

1976
'Actions Louder than Words'. Review of *A New Language for Psychoanalysis* by Roy Schafer. *NYRB*, 27 May.
'Warmth, Cant, and Gobbledegook'. Review of *Ordinary Ecstasy* by John Rowan. *TES*, 4 June.
'In Praise of Friendship'. Review of *Friends and Lovers* by Robert Brain. *New Society*, 28 October.
'Sickness of the Mind'. Review of *Breakdown* by Stewart Sutherland. *Observer*, 31 October.

1977
'Psychiatric Gambit'. Review of *Psychiatry on Trial* by Malcolm Lader. *New Society*, 4 August.
'Freud and His Heirs'. *Listener*, 27 October, and *Psychoanalysis and Beyond*, pp. 52–7.

1978
Introduction to *The Dissociation of a Personality: The Hunt for the Real Miss Beauchamp* by Morton Prince. Oxford: Oxford University Press, pp. v–xxi.
'The Way Madness Lies'. Review of *Reasoning about Madness* by J. K. Wing. *Observer*, 18 June.
'Will the Real Miss Beauchamp Please Stand Up?' (Abridgement of Introduction to *The Dissociation of a Personality*.) *New Society*, 9 November.

1979
The Innocence of Dreams. London: The Hogarth Press, and Oxford: Oxford University Press, 1981.
* 'Steps to an Ecology of Hope'. *The Sources of Hope*, ed. Ross Fitzgerald. Oxford: Pergamon Press, pp. 3–23. (Published in this volume as 'Faith, Hope and Charity'.)
'The Psyche and the Senses'. *How Does it Feel?*, ed. Mick Csaky. London: Thames & Hudson. See also *Psychoanalysis and Beyond*, pp. 159–66.
'Freud and Timpanaro'. *New Left Review*, 118, November/December and *Psychoanalysis and Beyond*, pp. 81–91.

1980
'How Psychosomatic is Your Illness?' Review of *Social Causes of Illness* by Richard Totman. *NYRB*, 3 April.
'Knowing the Worst Too Young'. Review of *Attachment and Loss*, vol. 3: *Loss, Sadness and Depression*, by John Bowlby. *New Society*, 13 March. See also *Psychoanalysis and Beyond*, pp. 147–55.
'A Very Rum Fellow Indeed'. Review of *Havelock Ellis: Philosopher of Sex* by Vincent Brome; *Havelock Ellis: A Biography* by Phyllis Grosskurth, and *Olive Schreiner* by Ruth First and Anne Scott. *TES*, 18 July.
'Sensuality from the Start'. Review of *Paedophilia: The Radical Case* by Tom O'Carroll and *The Story of Ruth* by Morton Schatzman. *TLS*, 21 November.

1981
'Back to the Old Adam'. Review of *The Red Lamp of Incest* by Robin Fox. *Observer*, 18 January.
'Not a Science'. Review of *The Case for a Personal Psychotherapy* by Peter Lomas. *New Society*, 16 July.

1982
'Orgone Recital'. Review of *Record of a Friendship: The Correspondence between Wilhelm Reich and A. S. Neill, 1936–1957*, ed. Beverley R. Placzek. *The Times*, 14 January.
'A New Look at Anti-psychiatry'. Review of *Psycho Politics* by Peter Sedgwick. *The Sunday Times*, 7 March.
'Variations on an Archetypal Theme'. Review of *Archetype: A Natural History of the Self* by Anthony Stevens. *New Society*, 20 May.
* 'Different Premises'. Review of *Freud and Jung: Conflicts of Interpretation* by Robert S. Steele. *THES*, 13 August. (Published in this volume as 'Why Freud and Jung Could Never Agree'.)
'How a Child Reacts to the Arrival of Baby'. Review of *Siblings: Love, Envy and Understanding* by Judy Dunn and Carol Kendrick. *New Society*, 11 November.
'Twilight States'. Review of *Dreams and How to Guide Them* by Hervey de Saint-Denys. *TLS*, 17 December.

1983
'Viewpoint: Analysis and the Autobiographer'. *TLS*, 27 May, and *Psychoanalysis and Beyond*, pp. 191–7.
'The Problems of Translating Freud'. Review of *Freud and Man's Soul* by Bruno Bettelheim. *New Society*, 14 July.
'Bedside Book'. Review of *The Oxford Book of Dreams*, ed. Stephen Brook. *New Society*, 20 October.
'What Analysts Say to Their Patients'. Unpublished lecture. First published in *Psychoanalysis and Beyond*, pp. 58–63.

1984
* 'A Case of Hysteria'. Review of *The Assault on Truth: Freud's Suppression of the Seduction Theory* by Jeffrey Moussaieff Masson. *NYRB*, 12 April, (Published in this volume as 'Masson's Assault on Freud'.)
'Psychoanalysis and Beyond'. Unpublished article. First published in *Psychoanalysis and Beyond*, pp. 119–27.

'Where I Came From'. Unpublished article, revised 1984. First published in *Psychoanalysis and Beyond*, pp. 198–206.

1985
Psychoanalysis and Beyond. London: Chatto & Windus.
'Images of War'. Review of *In a Dark Time*, ed. Nicholas Humphrey and Robert Jay Lifton. *New Society*, 17 January.
'A Hard Day's Night'. Review of *The Nightmare: The Psychology and Biology of Terrifying Dreams* by Ernest Hartmann. *N Y R B*, 28 March.
* 'Freud's Creative Illness'. Review of *The Complete Letters of Sigmund Freud to Wilhelm Fliess*, translated and edited by Jeffrey Moussaieff Masson. *N Y R B*, 30 May. (Published in this volume as 'A Passionate Friendship – Freud and Fliess'.)
* 'Symbolism, Imagination and Biological Destiny'. Lecture given as one of the Chichele Lectures at All Souls College, Oxford, in 1984, and published in *Freud and the Humanities* ed. Peregrine Horden. London: Duckworth.
* 'Where Is Psychoanalysis Going?' *Journal of the Royal Society of Medicine*, vol. 78.

1986
* 'Freudian Script'. Review of *The Freud Scenario* by Jean-Paul Sartre. *New Society*, 24 January. (Published in this volume as 'Sartre's Vision of Freud'.)
'The Sixth Sense'. Review of *The Man Who Mistook His Wife for a Hat and Other Clinical Tales* by Oliver Sacks. *N Y R B*, 13 March.
'Down to the Family.' Review of *Secrets of Strangers* by Alice Thomas Ellis and Tom Pitt-Aikens. *T L S*, 19 December.

1987
* 'More Psychohistory'. Review of *Freud for Historians* by Peter Gay. *Partisan Review*, no. 2. (Published in this volume as 'Freud for Historians'.)
* 'On Anxiety'. Unpublished lecture. (Published for the first time in this volume.)
* 'Remembering, Imagining, Creating'. Lecture given on 7 March 1987 at Mapperley Hospital, Nottingham, to a symposium on Creativity and Psychotherapy organized by the Nottingham Health Authortity Mental Illness Unit in conjunction with the West Midlands Institute of Psychotherapy. First published in *The Midland Journal of Psychotherapy*, December, no. 2.

1988
'Mirror Images'. Review of *The Self-Portrait: A Modern View* by Sean Kelly and Edward Lucie-Smith and *The Secret Surrealist: The Paintings of Desmond Morris* by Desmond Morris. *Modern Painters*, vol. 1, no. 1.

1990
* 'The Wound and the Bow'. Review of *Soul Murder: The Effects of Childhood Abuse and Deprivation* by Leonard Shengold. *N Y R B*, 1 March.
'Art on the Couch'. *Review of Sigmund Freud and Art: His Personal Collection of Antiquities*, ed. Lynn Gamwell and Richard Wells. *Modern Painters*, vol. 3, no. 1, Spring.
'Games Pollock Played'. *Review of Jackson Pollock: An American Saga* by Steven Naifeh and Gregory White Smith. *Modern Painters*, vol. 3, no. 2, Summer.

'Freud's Best Face'. Review of *Reading Freud: Explorations and Entertainments* by Peter Gay. *TLS*, 6 July.

'The Last Modern?' Review of *The Last Modern: A Life of Herbert Read* by James King. *Modern Painters*, vol. 3, no. 3.

* 'On Selfhood and Self-Awareness'. Unpublished essay. (Published for the first time in this volume.)

Index

Ablation of the Parental Images, On (Rycroft) 127, 157
Abraham, Karl 85
Action Language 120–1
Adam 142
Adolescence 156
All Souls College, Oxford 113
Anxiety 32–40
  anxiety dreams 35–8
  primary anxiety 38–40
  separation anxiety 35–8
  signal anxiety 38–9
Anxiety and Neurosis (Rycroft) 33–7
Auden, W. H. 114
Autism, Infantile 95–102, 157

Barker, Paul 5
Bartlett, Frederic 122, 130
Bateson, Gregory 4, 44
Beethoven, Ludwig van 128
Berne, Eric 2, 27
  Games People Play 108–10
Bettelheim, Bruno 2, 17, 95–102
  The Empty Fortress 95–102
  A Home for the Heart 95–102
  The Informed Heart 17, 95
Biological Destiny 122–4
Bonaparte, Marie 62–70, 75
Boston, Richard 5
Bowlby, John: *Attachment and Loss* 4, 39, 43, 80
Breuer, Josef 140
British Psycho-Analytical Society 1, 5
Buchenwald 95

Causes and Meaning (Rycroft) 6, 103
Charity 13–31
Charles II 24
Chekhov, Anton 87–9
Chicago Orthogenic School 96
Child abuse 71–81
Christian Church, Oxford Dictionary of 13
Christianity 13, 18, 23–4, 148
Clark, Ronald W.: *Freud: The Man and the Cause* 69
Cohen, John: *Humanistic Psychology* 17, 55
Collins, Wilkie: *Basil* 119
  The Moonstone 118–19
Coleridge, Samuel Taylor: *Kubla Khan* 128–30
Creative illness 67–8, 141
Creativeness 116–22, 126–32, 141, 147, 157–8
Critical Dictionary of Psychoanalysis (Rycroft) 32

Dachau 95
Darwin, Charles 131–2
Dean, James 25
Despair 11–31, 89, 99
Dickens, Charles 89
Disappointment 14–16
Dostoevsky, Feodor 87
Double bind 4, 44
Douglas, Mary: *Purity and Danger* 47

Eckstein, Emma 68, 76–7, 79
Eissler, K. R. 71

Eliot, George 2
Eliot, T. S. 4, 44, 119
Ellenberger, Henri F.: *The Discovery of the Unconscious* 67–8, 141
Envy 15, 151
Erikson, Erik H. 1, 16–22, 26, 83, 98
Eve 147
Exhibitionism 93
Existential analysis 114
Eysenck, Hans Jurgen 12

Fairbairn, W. R. D. 43
Faith 13–31, 89
Ferenczi, Sandor 77–9, 140
Confusion of Tongues between Adults and the Child 77–9
Fichte, Johann Gottleib 152
Fitzgerald, Ross: *The Sources of Hope* (ed.) 1, 5, 9
Fliess, Robert 66, 90–1
Fliess, Wilhelm 62–70, 74, 76, 90, 140–1
Freud and the Humanities ed. Peregrine Horden 113
Freud, Anna 4, 63–70, 71–2, 75, 138–41
Freud, Jakob 73
Freud, Martha 69
Freud, Martin 68
Freud, Sigmund 2, 17–18, 35–6, 38–9, 41–2, 50, 53–5, 59–61, 62–70, 71–9, 83, 89–91, 114–18, 121–4, 131, 138–41, 145, 151, 153–4
Aetiology of Hysteria, The 72–4, 90
Aus den Aufängen der Psychoanalyse 63
Civilization and its Discontents 39
Complete Letters of Sigmund Freud Wilhelm Fliess 62–70
Interpretation of Dreams, The 36
Origins of Psycho-Analysis 64–9
Project for a Scientific Psychology 62
Fuller, Peter 5

Gaea 128
Games theory 27–8, 106, 108–10
Gandhi, Mahatma 18

Gay, Peter: *Freud for Historians* 2, 82–5
Genesis 31, 126, 147
Geniuses 127–32, 136
Gestapo 63
God 13, 26, 91, 99, 126–7, 134, 143–5, 147–8, 156–7, 161
Goffman, Erving: *The Presentation of Self in Everyday Life* 27, 106
Gorer, Geoffrey 15
Gould, Tony 5
Green, André 120
Gross, John 5
Guéhenno, Jean: *Jean-Jacques Rousseau* 142–6
Guilt 155–6, 159

Halmos, Paul: *The Faith of the Counsellors* 26–7
Hauser, Kaspar 93
Hegel, Georg W. F. 3
Home H. J. 104
Hope 9–31
Hubris 156–62
Hume, David 3, 145
Husserl, Edmund 3
Huston, John: *Freud, the Secret Passion* (film) 138–41
Hysteria 49, 72–4, 90, 140

Idealism, Platonic 133
Idealization 21
Identity 152–3
Imagination 116–22, 129–32
Imagination and Reality (Rycroft) 21
Incest 93
Innocence of Dreams, The (Rycroft) 36, 158
Israëls, Han: *Schreber: Father and Son* 92

Jehovah 145
Jones, Ernest 44, 63–7, 71, 74, 82
Sigmund Freud: Life and Works 63–7, 82
Jung, Carl Gustav 42, 59–61, 114

Kafka, Franz 55
Kanner, Leo 92
Kaufman, Charles 139

Keynes, John Maynard: *Essays in Biography* 3
Kilmartin, Terence 5
King's Evil 24
Kipling, Rudyard 87–9, 157
Klein, Melanie 4, 42–3, 52, 114
Krafft-Ebing, Richard von 73
Kris, Ernst 63–5
Kris, Marianne 138

Lacan, Jacques 158
Laing, R. D. 114
Laslett, Peter 24
Lavin, Mary 129–30
Leopardi, Giacomo 21
Liddell, H. S. 39
Lowes, John Livingstone: *The Road to Xanadu* 128
Lowes Dickinson, Goldsworthy 3
Loyalty 156
Luther, Martin 18, 83
Luxembourg, Princesse de 144
Lynd, Helen Merrell: *On Shame and the Search for Identity* 85, 161

McDougall, William 11, 17
Mahler, Margaret 96
Malcolm, Janet: *In the Freud Archives* 72, 90, 92
Mansel, Henry Longueville 126
Marcuse, Herbert 105
Masson, Jeffrey Moussaieff 2, 62–70, 71–80, 90–1
    Assaulton Truth, The 71–80
    Against Therapy 71
    Complete Letters of Sigmund Freud to Wilhelm Fliess (ed.) 62–70
May, Rollo 114
Memory 122, 128–31
Metaphor 52, 121–2
Meynert, Theodor 140
Milner, Marion 122
Mitchell, James 5
Mnemosyne 128
Models in psychology 52, 115–19
Modern Painters 2, 147
Monroe, Marilyn 25, 138–41
Murdoch, Iris: *Sartre* 3

Narcissism 154–5
Narcissus 154

Neurosis, actual and psycho- 35
New Society 1
New Statesman 1
Newton, Isaac 128
New York Review of Books 1
Nietzsche, Friedrich 3

Observer 1
Oceanic Feeling 39
Oedipus Complex 138, 140
Oedipus Rex (Sophocles) 93
Orwell, George 87–8

Pathobiography 115–16
Perceval, Alicia C.: *Very Superior Men* 101
Philoctetes 86
Piaget, Jean 38
Pontalis J.-B. 138–41
Presley, Elvis 25
Prayer, Book of Common 24
Pride 161
Psychic apparatus 115
Psychoanalysis and Beyond (Rycroft) 3, 4, 9
Psychoanalysis Observed (Rycroft) 6
Psychosis 101
Psychosis, childhood 96

Rape, anal 93
Reinhart, Wolfgang 139
Richter, Jean-Paul 132
Rider Haggard, H. 157
Rie, Oscar 66–7
Rieff, Philip: *The Triumph of the Therapeutic* 27
Roazen, Paul 3, 82
Rolland, Romain 39
Rothschild Bank, Vienna 63
Rousseau, Jean-Jacques 142–6
Royal Society of Medicine 41
Ryle, Gilbert 120

St George's Hospital, London 32
Sartre, Jean-Paul 3, 133–7, 138–41
    The Freud Scenario 138–41
    Words 133–7
Sayers, Dorothy 119
Schafer, Roy 120

Schatzman, Morton: *Soul Murder: Persecution in the Family* 91–2
Schizophrenia 154
Schreber, Daniel Paul 91, 145, 153
  Memoirs of My Nervous Illness 91
Schreber, Moritz 91–2
Schur, Max: *The Specimen Dream of Psychoanalysis* 63, 68–9, 76
Schweitzer, Charles (Karl) 135
Seduction theory 70, 71–81, 90, 138
Self, Selfhood, Self-Awareness 14, 115, 147–162
Shame 155, 161–2
Shengold, Leonard: *Soul Murder: The Effects of Child Abuse and Deprivation* 2, 86–94
Silvers, Robert 5
Spinoza, Benedict 12
Stahl, Reinhold 62
Steele, Robert S.: *Freud and Jung: Conflicts of Interpretation* 59–61
Strachey, James 64
Sublimation 118, 129
Survival in extreme situations 86–102
Symbolism 44, 121–4, 131
Szasz, Thomas 2, 61, 103–7, 108–9, 120

  Ideology and Insanity 103
  Myth of Mental Illness, The 103

Thring, Edward 101
Times Literary Supplement, The 1
Trilling, Lionel: *Sincerity and Authenticity* 158
Trust, basic 16–18

Uranus 128

Vigilance 33–8
Vinci, Leonardo da 128
Virtues, Theological 9–31
Virtue (an ego-strength) 18–19
Vision, Beatific 16

War, First World 28
Warhol, Andy 15
Will 131
Wilson, Edmund: *The Wound and the Bow* 86
Winnicott, D. W. 2, 4, 42–5, 52, 80, 96, 100
Wordsworth, William: *Lyrical Ballads*; *The Prelude* 129

Young-Bruehl, Elisabeth: *Anna Freud: A Biography* 138